Craft Your Own Wish Quilt

Craft your wishes into reality—make an enchanting quilted talisman that radiates the positive energy of your own magical goals!

Magical fabric art is a fulfilling, creative way to invite more magic into your home. You'll learn how to combine fabrics, gems, herbs, colors, and even aromas into a lovely piece of handcrafted art that will radiate the power of your visualizations and wishes.

Make your talisman large or make it small. Keep it simple or lavish it with detail. Instead of limiting your creativity with set patterns and traditional quilting rules, *Magical Fabric Art* will inspire you to fashion a one-of-a-kind magical heirloom.

Could your life benefit from a little more love and healing ... a measure of harmony ... a shot of energy? Your quilt will act as a dynamic talisman for positive change. Choose the colors that magically enhance your purpose ... tuck special herbs into secret pockets to increase your emotional readiness for change ... stitch on gemstones that emanate rays of invisible energy ... sprinkle with aromas to heal and stimulate ... and inscribe with powerful symbols used throughout the ages by the wise.

By stitching together these earthy ingredients, leavened by wishes and the loving care of your hands, you can make true magic.

About the Author

Sandra McCraw Scarpa has had a life-long interest in the nature mysteries and has read, studied, and traveled during her adult life to pursue knowledge on these subjects.

She shares her interests, talents, and extensive library with her daughter, Lark, who writes on Wiccan and New Age subjects, as well. Sandra, with her daughter, Lark, have written a New Age/Wiccan romance novel, *Flames of Rapture* and a novella, *Trick or Treat*.

To Write to the Author

If you wish to contact the author or would like more information about this book, please write to the author in care of Llewellyn Worldwide and we will forward your request. Both the author and the publisher appreciate hearing from you and learning of your enjoyment of this book and how it has helped you. Llewellyn Worldwide cannot guarantee that every letter written to the author can be answered, but all will be forwarded. Please write to:

Sandra McCraw Scarpa
c/o Llewellyn Worldwide
P.O. Box 64383, Dept. K653-X
St. Paul, MN 55164-0383, U.S.A.

Please enclose a self-addressed, stamped envelope for reply, or $1.00 to cover costs. If outside U.S.A., enclose international postal reply coupon.

Magical Fabric Art

Spellwork and Wishcraft Through Patchwork Quilting and Sewing

Sandra McCraw Scarpa

1998
Llewellyn Publications
St. Paul, Minnesota 55164-0383, U.S.A.

FIRST EDITION
First Printing, 1998

Cover design: Anne Marie Garrison
Cover talisman: Becca Allen
Interior illustrations: Helen Michaels
Calligraphy in chapter three: Tamami Nakaseko
Book design and editing: Astrid Sandell
Photography (insert page 1): Sandra McCraw Scarpa
Photography (cover and insert page 2-4): Doug Deutscher
Photographic insert design: Lisa Novak
Information in Chapter 13 reprinted with permission from The NAMES
    Project Foundation

Library of Congress Cataloging-in-Publications Data
Scarpa, Sandra McCraw, 1941-
    Magical Fabric Art : spellwork and wishcraft through patchwork
    quilting and sewing / Sandra McCraw Scarpa. — 1st ed.
        p.   cm.
    Includes bibliographical references and index.
    ISBN 1-56718-653-X (trade paper)
    1. Patchwork. 2. Quilting. 3. Talismans. I. Title.
    TT835.S279   1998   98-3384
    746.46—dc21   CIP

Publisher's Note: Llewellyn Worldwide does not participate in, endorse, or have any authority or responsibility concerning private business transactions between our authors and the public.

    All mail addressed to the author is forwarded but the publisher cannot, unless specifically instructed by the author, give out an address or phone number.

Llewellyn Publications
A Division of Llewellyn Worldwide, Ltd.
P.O. Box 64383, Dept. K653-X
St. Paul, Minnesota 55164-0383, U.S.A.

Printed in the U.S.A.

Also by Sandra McCraw Scarpa

Flames of Rapture (with Lark Eden, Leisure Love Spell, 1996)
Trick or Treat, novella (with Lark Eden, Leisure Love Spell, 1997)

Contents

Crafting Personal Talismans

He who knows what sweets and virtues are in the ground, the plants, the waters, the heavens, and how to come at these enchantments—is the rich and royal man.

—Ralph Waldo Emerson

*T*he astral world, the world we cannot see but only intuit, is most closely touched by us in the things that affect the human senses. Ephemeral things such as fragrances, colors, textures, dreams, and memories are our windows to the other world. By blending these gossamer materials with our conscious will, we can produce the effect called magic.

In this book, I suggest construction materials and simple methods for quilt-like talismans that will aid your psychological well-being by helping to produce harmony, love, health, energy, and protection.

Producing a handmade quilted talisman actualizes a powerful aura of sympathetic magic, a channel to the vortex of supernatural forces that is within our own capabilities to harness. Forging a tool with your own hands devises an end result with energy of its own, the sum greater than the disparate parts. By helping you to focus your personal power of creativity and desire toward a specific goal, the construction can bring about change in your inner and outer life.

Who doesn't remember the peaceful feeling of being wrapped in a warm quilt on a cold night? It was as if the person who made the coverlet was there, wrapping you in love and caring. There is something of the person who made the blanket within the threads and fabrics. The cloth could be worn soft as the hands that made the stitches; just touching the patches could bring back a picture memory and the emotion of love. The handiwork creates something entirely unique and personal, a child of your hands.

Love is the power that fuels the intent.

—Lark Eden

Chapter 1

Selecting and Preparing Your Materials

Supplies for a Collage of Wishes Made Visible

All hand made objects contain a bit of energy. The process that creates these objects is more than a simple repetition of techniques. During the creation process the craftsperson, through concentration and the physical activity involved, moves energy from within the body, through the hands, and into the material being worked.

—Scott Cunningham

All magic is contained within the wishful intent. Love is the power that fuels the actions, and love is the greatest power we can summon. Hope, love, joy, grief—the extremes of human feelings can be portrayed in the traditional medium of quilting. How many dreams and wishes have been stitched into the weaves of quilts made for weddings, new babies, or young people about to embark upon a new life? The touch of familiar cloth has soothed the pain of the makers of memory quilts who stitch to ease the transit of sorrow as they grieve.

A unique aspect of magical talisman quilts is the incorporation of natural amulets of herbs, flowers, stones, and scents. The use of these substances is a part of earth magic, a power that taps into the rhythm and force of Nature. Some say the power is not symbolic, but very real, a vibration of natural energy that is attuned to the associated need.

A crimson rose for love. Salt for purification and protection. Sugar to draw the sweetness of wealth. The green fire of an emerald to give peace and emotional healing. An elegantly simple Chinese ideogram for harmony, *ho*, to remind us that wisdom and stillness bring order in the world. The pungent scent of eucalyptus for healing, or the spice of carnations for energy. Alirazin red cloth to give strength of will and energy.

Sew, paint, glue, draw—be passionate about your dreams and wishes and express them freely. Feel free to paint the symbols of your wish on the cloth, write on the fabric, stencil symbols, letters, or pictures, sew bits of memories to the whole: a train ticket, a note from a fortune cookie, a ribbon from a treasured gift, a button from your lover's shirt. The traditional craft of tiny stitches and frugality can be turned upside down and inside out to reach an expression of humanity wrought with our hands, memories, and a few physical artifacts. Open your heart and hands and let your imagination fly. This is your creation, a collage of wishes made whole and visible.

Visualization is defined in *Webster's Dictionary* as "To make or become visible; to see or form a mental image." See your creative prayer fulfilled in your mind's eye throughout construction. Only kind thoughts filled with good and positive purposes should be visualized: good health, love, energy, harmony, and peace. Visualization by the maker while assembling the cloth blesses the materials and the finished product with the power of inspiration.

Shakti Gawain clearly explains the technique of symbolic intentions in her book *Creative Visualization* (Bantam New Age, 1985). She reviews the three key elements within your personality that will work for you in a situation involving linking your imagination with the real in order to produce concrete results. These elements are:

Desire: Ask yourself, "Do I truly desire this goal in my heart?"

Belief: The more you believe in your goal, the higher the possibility of obtaining it.

Acceptance: Sometimes we pursue a goal simply for the process of the pursuit, never really picturing the end product. Ask yourself, "Am I willing to possess this goal?"

Gawain adds: "The sum total of these three elements is . . . your intention. When you have total intention to create something—that is you deeply desire it, you completely believe that you can do it, and you are totally willing to have it—it simply cannot fail to manifest."

Visualization is not wishing. By creating a picture, an image of what is to be, you create a focus for the natural forces you can awaken. Hold a magnifying glass in the sun— it is, after all, only glass. Add plain sunlight and focus it on a piece of paper. In a second, there is smoke, then flames as the glass channels the invisible energy and creates action.

The ability to visualize is an important one in the use of creative positive magic. This is why pictures, symbols, words, and charms are important. They direct our mental concentration, imprinting the energy and guiding the force to a destination—the destination we choose. The careful choice of herbs, flowers, aromas, stones, and colors adds and strengthens the magical dimensions of the talisman.

Pictures, symbols, and words direct our mental energies and guide forces to a destination.

The quilts do not have to be the neatly patched productions of our grandmothers. They should be a work of your heart, from your heart, and as such should be free from criticism and constraint. There are many ways to produce a work such as these quilts. It is the desire of the maker that is important and the product, what we will call the quilt, a tangible symbol of that desire.

What Skills Do I Need?

Expert sewing talent is not needed for these talismans. Only the simplest cutting and sewing is required. The finished projects gain artistic vitality from the combinations of materials— fabrics, colors, objects, pictures, patterns. The art term *collage* most accurately describes the appearance of these talismans.

The basic skills needed are the ability to thread and use a plain sewing needle. A simple, even, in-and-out stitch—a

A running stitch, as shown above, is a simple, even, in-and-out stitch that is easy to use for both construction of your talisman and in decorative stitching.

running stitch (see above)—is all that is called for, even for the decorative stitching. A sewing machine may be used for the construction if one is available, but it is not necessary.

Use sharp scissors and new needles to reduce frustration and produce a worthy product. A common mistake is using old, dull blades that have been used to cut everything from newspaper to spinach stems. Use small to medium size needles that are easy for you to thread and handle, not giant fat spikes.

There are many books on easy quiltmaking available in stores and libraries. Although you will not be constructing an actual "quilt," the sewing methods and suggestions for fabric handling presented in these manuals will be instructive and helpful if you are inexperienced.

Do I Have to Follow a Pattern?

No. If you remember your mother or grandmother struggling with tiny pieces of paper pinned to cloth, please be reassured that you won't have to submit yourself to this frustrating task.

I use "crazy quilting" or a "quick log cabin" construction for my work, as these designs are easily assembled and are adaptable to use of all types, sizes, and textures of cloth scraps.

Crazy quilting is a pattern without a pattern. It simply starts around a small central panel or area and continues to grow, much as a flower's petals open. The variety in colors, shapes, and materials make a richly complex design unfold from an extremely simple method. This technique easily accommodates different textures and types of fabrics used in the same piece.

The simplest patch-over-patch of the "Crazy Quilt" was a Victorian favorite derived from an ancient Japanese method, *yosegire*, which means "the sewing together of different fragments." Historically, Asian fabric—both bolts and items of clothing—inspired a love and reverence that bordered on the spiritual. Techniques of weaving, sewing, and fabric embellishment took on a magical significance in the Orient.

By "patching" fabric together, the life of the precious textile is prolonged. In this way, honor is given to the maker and implies the hope of long life for the recipient of the patchwork. The number of patches in an item often matches the age of the recipient of the gift, especially on auspiciously significant birthdays such as the seventy-seventh, eighty-eighth, or ninety-ninth.

This crazy-patch technique was not limited to Japan. A similar form arose in Korea. It was believed that organizing the scraps of cloth into a thing of beauty brought spiritual happiness to both the maker and the recipient of the gift. One of the earliest uses mentioned for this type of cloth was as wrapping for the sacred Buddhist *sutras*.

The "log cabin" method, illustrated below, starts in the center of the quilt, with a central square. Each "log" is a strip of cloth that builds in a 1-2-3-4 fashion around the edges.

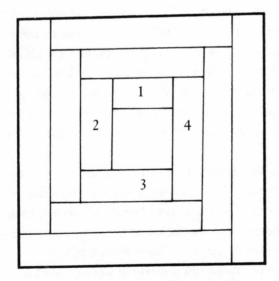

The log cabin quilt pattern builds a simple square radiating from a center panel by adding strips of the same width in the order indicated in this illustration.

If you are an accomplished seamstress or skillful maker of regular quilts, a traditional pattern with personal or popular meaning could be used. For example, in the elegant "Double Wedding Ring," the interlocking rings of love and eternity could be expressed in the love-drawing colors of pinks and reds for a magic love quilt. A fiery burst of a "Lone Star" in yellows, oranges, and other energy bringing colors would be magnificent for an energy quilt. There are more than 3,000 traditional designs for patchwork quilts.

Many of us are familiar with the Amish quilts, which are valued for the naive artistic merit of simplistic but powerful graphic art statements. Dark solid colors—set off, bordered with, and incorporating deep black—project a mystic vigor of forceful undiluted colors. Their power is derived from the calm, lovingly centered hands that produce the quilts, sewing in the energy and drawing down the quality wished for. The quilts made for a specific person or family are more potent that those made for sale because they are created with a loving target of intent in mind.

How Much Will This Cost and Where Should I Get My Materials?

The cost of a magic quilt can be as much as you wish to invest in materials—or as little. Size is a variable quality—a rather small quilt can be made if you choose to use expensive stones or fabrics. Items used on and in the quilt are usually found objects, things that you already have around the house—old clothes, jewelry, plants and herbs, greeting cards, small mementos, personal drawings, or gifts. Items that should be new may be used in small quantity if price is a factor.

Finding the things that you need is usually a matter of a thoughtful walk through your house. As you think of your need, objects will come to your hand: a photo of a friend in a happy time, a note someone wrote to encourage you, a ticket stub, a pressed flower, or a ribbon from a gift.

Cloth may come from something worn or used by you or the person you are sewing for. Used clothing from a second-hand shop or an unknown source should be avoided as the fabric may carry the previous owner's sad overtones and bad memories. Incorporating satin from a bride's gown, worn denim of a favorite pair of jeans, a special t-shirt, or perhaps a glove worn by a lover or friend will all bring unique endowments to the quilt.

You can purchase new cloth in colors and patterns needed to represent qualities you are wishing for at fabric and craft shops. For example, cloth for a love quilt might include designs of red roses, hearts, and ribbons. Small lengths of less than a yard are usually inexpensive. The total amount spent for materials, including stones, will probably be less than $20.

Endeavor to use natural materials—those from the earth— such as light cotton or linen fabric. Wool, although natural, can be heavy, thick, and difficult to handle. It also shrinks and carries an odor. Purists might add that the animal fiber implies a certain sense of exploitation, as well. Synthetics— such as polyester, nylon, and plastic—have no natural energies and lack the ability to retain any energy you wish to project into them.

How Big Should My Magic Quilt Be?

Size is not important. The "quilt" may be as small as an 8-inch by 11-inch magazine cover, as compact as a bandana, as big as an afghan, or as generous as a regular-sized blanket.

Size is a decision for the craftsperson to make—there is no set size or shape of a wish quilt. Do not worry if your creation is not perfectly square or rectangular—an irregular shape adds visual interest and life to the work. Because you will begin to work from the center of the quilt outward to the edge, the size of your project can be adjusted. After you have added all components, the edges can be trimmed straight, taking off an inch or several inches if necessary. Structurally, the backing of the piece will help keep the quilt intact.

For simplicity, I give a general example of cutting and constructing on a base of 45-inch square muslin, the general size of an afghan or baby blanket, because that is an easy size to prepare and work with. You might find it easier to use a smaller piece for your first creation—the first magic quilt I made was the size of a man's handkerchief.

Items that are applied to the surface of the fabric are called embellishments. An embellishment could be a ribbon, bell, button, dried flower, small stuffed animal, letter, card, or any item with personal meaning to you. Embellishments can be sewn, glued, or tied on; they can dangle, jingle, sparkle, flutter. The articles give artistic flair and deepen the personal imagery within the construction.

How Shall I Use My Magic Quilt?

This magic collage can be used as a banner, wall hanging, lap robe, nap cover, or bed quilt. A finished flat assembly can be re-cut and sewn into a striking vest or jacket. The work could be framed, made into a pillow top, or tucked away as a special keepsake. The purposeful goal behind the construction is uppermost, not a display of artistic or sewing skill.

Whether the articles are meant to attract or repel as a talisman or amulet, magic quilts are an aid to strengthen your psychological self-assurance. One definition of magic is "an act of will that brings about purposeful changes in your personal environment." The intent and purpose of your act brings about the magic in your life as much as the act itself.

A talisman is an object charged with natural power to attract a specific energy or force to its maker and owner. The word *talisman* is derived from the Greek *teleo*, meaning "to consecrate." A talisman is prepared for a definite purpose and may be carried, worn, or put in a specific public or private place. Another term for such an article would be *charm*.

An amulet is generally meant to deflect or repel a specific energy, such as a negative force. The word *amulet* comes from a Latin term meaning "an object that protects a person from trouble." While an amulet may be naturally endowed with magical properties, a talisman is aimed, charged, or energized specifically for its objective.

Harm, evil, or negativity should never be projected into magic quilts. Never forget the Threefold Rule—that what is given will return threefold to the giver—and always keep in mind the prime principle of "Harm none."

As you select the fabrics, colors, herbal inclusions, stitching patterns, and fragrances, positive thoughts should

be uppermost in your mind. The power of your intent—
your goal—is what you are creating and bringing to a
material form.

When Should I Start Making My Quilt?

Consult your calendar to select the lunar phase that will aid
your project. For instance, all projects involving protection
should, optimally, be done in the period of time when the
moon is waxing (growing). The increase of the lunar disk
symbolizes the growth of your confidence and security.

However, knowing modern time schedules and constraints,
at least start during the waxing time, and if the length of time
spills into the next lunar phase, adjust in a positive manner the
visualization and intention you are projecting. Again using
protection as an example, if construction runs over into the
waning phase, picture the evil influences losing their power or
negative forces melting away as the moon becomes dark.

Each chapter will express the beneficial lunar phase and
day for your selected purpose. Briefly, these are:

Love: Friday, Moon in sign of Cancer, waxing Moon

Inner harmony: Monday, full or new Moon

Protection: Tuesday, waxing Moon drawing increase
of security

Energy: Sunday, waxing Moon producing fullness
of vitality

Healing: Wednesday, waning Moon if visualization is
for affliction to diminish, waxing Moon if good health
is increasing

How Long Will a Project Take?

One project, made to a 45-inch by 45-inch size, usually takes
me one lunar month (28 to 30 days) to complete. Naturally,
a construction of this type that requires your mental focus
and not just your physical presence cannot be hurried. Daily
life makes its demands, so do not be discouraged if the creation of your quilt takes longer than you anticipate. But,
once you begin, make certain to finish!

There are several stages to be completed before beginning to actually sew the quilt: preparing a workbox, empowering the cloth, pinning the batting and backing, making a preliminary arrangement of materials, and so forth. I suggest treating each of these steps as "one day's work." Plan a time each day when you can work undisturbed and concentrate on your project without interruptions. Do not rush through any part of your task.

Where Shall I Keep My Supplies?

Cloth and other supplies should be kept in a box with a top or lid. This container should not be used for any other purpose and should be kept closed when not in use. While your work is unfinished, the potential and personality of the talisman is growing and coming into being. The protection of the container will keep negative vibrations from attacking or inhabiting the unfinished quilt. The shelter will seal and nurture the intentions you wish to foster within the handwork.

A basket is not good for this use; the slatted weave has holes that permit escape and egress of energy. I prefer a new white gift box or other carton that has not been previously used.

To cleanse a container to use as your workbox, sprinkle a generous handful of sea salt in the box. Dust and sift the salt grains around the receptacle as if dusting a cake pan. Leave the open box and salt in sunlight for three days. After three days have passed, turn the container upside down over a clean sheet of white paper and pat the bottom to remove the used salt. Close the box.

Fold the paper carefully to enclose all salt grains and dispose of the paper and salt in an area away from your house. Your workbox is now cleaned and prepared for the project in progress or for safe storage of the finished talisman.

Keep your materials gathered in an orderly manner in the box when you are not using them. If possible, store your workbox beneath your bed when you are not working on the talisman. This will put deeper personal vibrations into the materials—as you sleep, your unconscious is busy with symbolic suggestions for your creative mind. You will know which thoughts are magical power symbols and should be included.

What Should I Include on My List of Materials?

These are the general items that will be needed. Specific designs, colors, and articles for quilts with different magical properties are described in each chapter.

- new muslin or patterned cloth for the construction base (backing): approximately 1½ yards
- new cloth in motifs and colors chosen for significance to your personal purpose
- candles
- potpourri or incense ingredients
- kettle for potpourri or incense
- large non-metallic pot for cloth preparation
- new wooden spoon
- herbs
- oils
- stones
- safety pins (one inch long)
- thread, needles, straight pins
- thin batting such as Thermolam or flannel: approximately 1½ yards
- personal amulets such as ribbons, buttons, pictures
- black indelible ink, laundry marker, or ⅛ yard black cloth
- Wonderunder or other fabric bonding film: ½ yard
- chalk or sliver of soap

I'm Ready to Begin. How Shall I Start?

The single most important thing for effective talisman construction is to have a clear idea of what you wish to accomplish. You should be able to write this in a single sentence, such as:

"I need more physical energy."

"I want more love in my life."

"I wish to increase the quality of my inner life by restoring harmony within."

"I desire to increase my feelings of security by shielding myself from the negative forces that surround me."

When you have clarified your goal and are able to express the objective in a brief, positive manner, you are ready to begin. Write your desire clearly on a clean sheet of white paper. Seal the written declaration in a clean, new white envelope. Use the envelope as a place marker in this book until your workbox is prepared. Touching this note to yourself as you read will remind you of your goal. When your workbox is ready, place the envelope on the bottom of the container.

Each day, give your total attention to each task, no matter how ordinary the chore.

Read the chapter concerning the purpose of your magic quilt closely, then make a list of the materials you need. Construction goes smoothly when all items—fabrics, stones, herbs, photos, and so on—are assembled before beginning the composition.

A dedication, or beginning ritual, will be suggested for use before embarking on each project. This will help you focus your thoughts and energy on the most important aspect of the creation of this work: the intent.

Before beginning any project that involves your spiritual concentration, it is wise to purify yourself—both symbolically and in reality. Take a bath and meditate on your purpose, using the recommended herbs, flowers, and stones for your project as aids. See the water washing away your sad or negative feelings. Burn a white candle for peace of spirit, and take up the spell of kind labor when you are relaxed and centered into the work. The great saint Teresa of Lisieux called this "the prayer of the hands"—being in and with the physical work of your body so that a spiritual result is woven in harmony with your thoughts. Her credo stated that each day of your life you should give your total attention to each task, no matter how ordinary the chore. Whatever you do should be done with the knowledge that the task is in harmony with the universe, which brings peace and balance into your life.

The visualization of what you are requesting must be held uppermost in your mind when you are constructing any kind of magic wish quilt. Choose a time for your activities that will allow you to use your labor as an aid to meditation—a time without interruptions or distractions. Focus on your end desire to be accomplished by this quilt talisman. If your mind is not on your handiwork, if you cannot pick up your cloth in a good and positive spirit, then leave the construction in the workbox for the time being.

How Do I Prepare My Fabric?

Charging is one of the processes of empowering, the act of moving energy into an object. You may charge cloth by steeping (soaking) it in pure water and a selection of herbs. Use a porcelain, enamel, or glass (like Pyrex or Corning) pot and stir with a new wooden spoon. Do not use a metal pot or spoon—the metal may react chemically in an undesirable way.

If the beginning of your project is blessed by a thunderstorm, collect rainwater to use for charging your cloth or for preparing gem elixirs. Rainwater collected in a thunderstorm gives the best intensification of desired energy, as does fresh seawater. If a thunderstorm is not available, draw water on a sunny day at noon, when the Sun is at its peak. You may use bottled unpure, noncarbonated spring water, if you wish.

Fill an enamel or glass vessel with pure water. The size of the pot will vary according to the amount of cloth you wish to charge. My charging pots are large white enamel stock pots, which each hold two gallons of liquid. Cloth should be able to float freely and not be crammed in.

Add a double handful of sea salt to the cold water. Measure with your hands, not a cup. Swirl the salt into the water by moving your hands in a clockwise direction until the salt is completely dissolved. Picture your intentions entering the liquid as the salt does. As you stir the water, visualize the change that you desire. To make that transformation occur, mentally push energy into the water. See your palms and fingers spreading your personal internal power. Imagine a dynamic current flowing from your fingertips into the water.

*Steep fabric for a
love talisman in
red rose petals,
rosemary, and yarrow.*

Add three generous pinches each of three of the herbs selected for the desired properties. A pinch is roughly a tablespoon, or as much as you can gather between the bunched five fingertips of one hand. Crush the plant matter lightly with your fingers as you sprinkle the leaves and flowers into the water in a clockwise motion.

As the faint fragrance rises, think of the aroma surrounding you with an aura of peace and reassurance, and the quality you are requesting. As an example, I used new cloth steeped with red rose petals, rosemary and yarrow—which were all grown in pots on my porch—for a love talisman.

Gently stir the mixture in a clockwise direction, to follow the practice of moving in a sunwise manner (from the left to the right, or the direction a clock hand moves). This is an appropriate ritual direction for positive magic.

Slowly bring the liquid to a boil. Allow the water to simmer for three, seven, or nine minutes. Remove the pot from the heat and allow to cool completely.

As a practical and aesthetic consideration, treat groups of the same hue-intensity cloth together, so that any dark dyes will not discolor your light fabrics. I separate the colors as I would for my usual wash—light colors with light, dark with dark. I have two pots, one for dark cloth and one for light colors. The salt will aid in fixing any color that has a tendency to run or bleed.

Simple charging, as described above, is sufficient for transfer of magic from plant to cloth. Charging usually does not change the color of the cloth to any great degree. A patterned or colored fabric may be charged without destroying the aesthetic appeal.

Although natural dyeing can be time consuming, beautiful and subtle tints can be produced using plain cotton muslin dyed with strong infusions of the herbs and plants selected for the powers needed. The colors imparted may not be those you expect, but the powers of the plants represented would be symbolically transferred to the fabric. Generally, the natural hues are pale unless aided by mordants such as alum, copper salts, or other agents.

Some herbs and flowers are powerful in their magic qualities, but their odors may not be as appealing to our noses.

For instance, onion and garlic are powerful herbs for defense, but will not make your cloth smell very pleasant. Better to invoke their power by having a nice dish of spaghetti—vegetarian style—before requesting defensive aid.

New fabrics come folded in half on the bolt. Unfold the cloth to be empowered and shake it out vigorously so that there are no tight folds. Immerse the fabric in plain pure water. Swish the textiles in the water until the threads are completely saturated. Using your hands, gently squeeze out excess liquid.

Place the wet fabric into the cooled, infused water. Lift the material up and down several times using the wooden spoon and make certain that all the cloth is wet. Leave the fabric in the pot to steep overnight. If possible, place the pot outside in the moonlight, making certain to protect it from animals or children.

The next day, rinse the fabric thoroughly by hand or run the cloth through the wash cycle without soap to remove bits of plant matter and eliminate any possible allergic reaction from the herbs and salt. You may notice small spots of color where the woven material has come into direct contact with a leaf or flower. This is not a problem.

Allow the cloth to dry in the moonlight before using, and finally, press the fabric carefully before cutting or sewing.

Cut new fabric to size after any herbal treatment has been carried out and the cloth has been pressed. If you choose not to steep the cloth with herbs, wash and press the material well before beginning. This act makes the cloth yours.

After fabric has been washed and pressed, the threads often draw into a "true" position, which changes the shape of the cloth somewhat. Pieces that you intend to use as strips or patches on the front of the quilt may be left as they are until you are ready to put them into position. After you have decided where they should go, the patches may be trimmed into the shape or size you need.

The cloth you have selected and charged to use as the backing may be trimmed to an even square or rectangle for ease of handling and construction. Unfold the cloth you have selected for the backing. Trim the lower end straight and square. If you have a problem deciding how to make a sharp

90-degree square corner, place the corner of a book or magazine at the edge of the cloth and align the margin of the cloth with the edge of the cover. Make a light mark with soap, chalk or pencil to guide your scissors (below).

To prepare to cut the cloth to your desired size, first trim the lower end square. You may wish to use the edge of a book or other 90° angle to trace a perfect square edge. Place the bottom of the book along woven (*selvage*) edge of cloth.

Cut on the marked line (page 17, top).

Smooth the cloth down with your hands. Have the edge that you have just trimmed at the bottom. Take the lower right corner and fold it up to the diagonal upper left corner of the other side. This will make a triangle that will become a perfect square when unfolded. Unfold to check that you have done this correctly before cutting! Cut across the width (page 17, bottom).

This square will become the base of the attachments for the quilt, as well as the back of the quilt. Most fabric is 45 to 46 inches in width; your square will be about a 45-inch square. Dimensions are not exact due to the nature of fabric; cloth "draws up" or stretches, new and used fabrics are of different textures, techniques used will pull or fold cloth, and so on. I refer to this piece of cloth, with the batting pinned to it, as the backing.

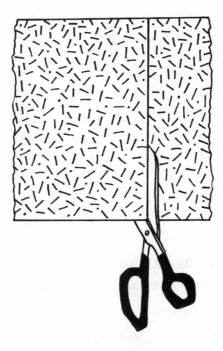

Following the mark you've made to indicate a square corner, cut a straight edge on your fabric.

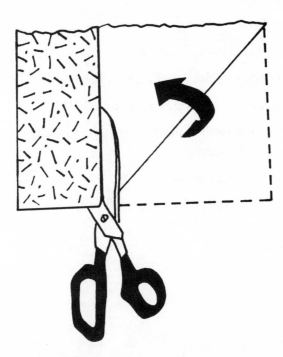

To cut a square, fold the lower right corner of your fabric to meet the upper left corner. Cutting along the line of this triangle will provide a square piece to work with.

The same square-cutting process is done for a piece of thin batting such as Thermolam or white flannel so that the batting is the same size as the backing muslin. Thermolam and flannel generally are 45 inches in width. If flannel is used, wash the fabric in very hot water before cutting in order to soften the cloth. Thermolam or regular cotton quilt batting does not need pre-treatment. If all-polyester Thermolam is used, unfold the batting and allow it to relax overnight before using.

After all construction is completed, the quilt should not be washed.

Please Give Me a Quick Summary of Charging and Preparing the Cloth

1. Collect water.

2. Add sea salt and swirl with your right hand.

3. Add herbs and stones.

4. Simmer.

5. Cool.

6. Wet cloth and squeeze out.

7. Add wet cloth to charged water.

8. Steep cloth overnight in moonlight.

9. Rinse cloth in plain water to remove any excess salt and herbs.

10. Dry cloth in moonlight.

11. Iron cloth and store in workbox.

Chapter 2

Composition, Construction, and Finishing

Intent and Purpose United in a Physical Result

By small actions
Accomplishing great things.

—Tao 63

*B*efore beginning any aspect of your magical work, read the complete chapter related to the purpose you wish to pursue. You will, in fact, find it helpful to read all of the chapters, in order to acquaint yourself with the techniques used and to add elements of other requests beneficial to your task.

I Have Everything Selected and Prepared. Can I Begin?

Press the backing fabric and lay it out—right side *down*—on a large table or other flat surface. A clean floor will do, but be advised that your cat will love this part of the process and help you by sitting in the center of the fabric. Smooth the batting or flannel over the backing fabric. The batting should match in size, or be slightly larger. There should be no wrinkles or folds (see diagram on page 20, top).

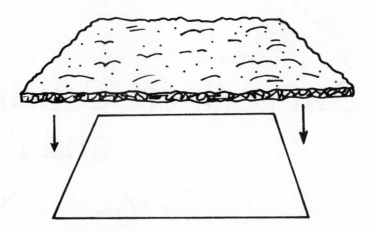

Place the batting material over the backing fabric. The batting should match in size or be slightly larger.

Pinning is a basic construction technique that will allow you to handle, fold, and otherwise move the quilt without everything falling apart. Using plenty of large (1 inch long) safety pins, pin the backing and batting together. Use a pin about every 4 to 6 inches (shown below). Straight pins can't be used as they are a hazard while you work because they scratch and fall out. The safety pins will be removed as you add the components of the quilt.

Use safety pins to join your batting and backing together. Place pins about 4 to 6 inches apart.

When the backing and the batting are pinned together, you have made the base for your quilt. Fold the assembly in half, then in half again, creating four simple folds. Add one colored pin or a small mark at the center point fold, so that you can use the pin as a point of location as you construct the quilt top.

Now that your fabric backing and batting is pinned together and marked, you can pick it up, loosely fold it, and store the base in your workbox.

How Do I Choose a Pleasing Layout?

Spread the pinned batting and backing cloth flat. Lay out the components that you have selected to include. For instance, you may have a scarf, a photograph, a t-shirt, flowers, a ring or pin, a letter or card, or other small items. You will also have fabric in the colors and motifs that you have picked to empower your wish.

Start at the center of the quilt. Arrange your central motif first, then lay the fabric you have chosen around the central panel, until the edge of the backing is reached. Does it seem that there will be enough fabric to cover the total area you wish? It may be necessary to add a wider border or more pieces. Next, lay amulets, embellishments, and other cloth on the fabric until you reach a satisfactory artistic balance. Don't pin or fasten anything down yet. Just move the pieces around and think.

This process will help you get a picture of how the construction process will proceed: from the center outward.

Do not add the herbal inclusions until you are at the point where they may be immediately secured into the quilt. For instance, do not sprinkle in salt or flower petals until you are prepared to sew down that section and enclose the substances.

Borders are strips that are sewn around the edge of the quilt to enclose the total work. Artistically, borders add a framed look or a finish to the construction (see page 22, top).

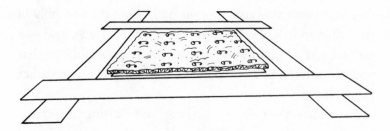

Borders, strips sewn around the edges of the quilt, provide a framed, finished look for your construction.

The width of borders is up to you, but 3 to 6 inches is good (see diagram below). Cut cloth at least ½ inch wider than the width needed and 6 inches longer than the length needed to give yourself room, *allowance*, for seams or to change your mind as you plan your composition.

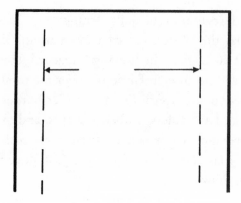

Cut fabric for borders at least ½ inch wider than the width of your quilt, and 6 inches longer than the length.

When you are ready to begin working with the fabric pieces, first lay the cloth where you wish on the prepared batting and backing, then place the embellishments on top. When the patches are sewn together, they will be a bit smaller due to the loss of the cloth included in the seams.

Arrangement of the components often takes several days as you work to reach a satisfactory artistic balance. In creating my quilt tops, I decide what will be the center starting motif, and that is the first cloth or item that is placed. Then,

I lay out the other pieces and shift and change them. When I reach a point where I like the form, I cover the pieces with a light cloth to prevent things from being disturbed and leave the quilt overnight.

The next day, I look to see if the composition still pleases me, that colors and textures are balanced, and the elements meet the requirements for magical structure. The quilt should project a pleasing overall organization. Often after a night's rest, an obvious "hole" in the arrangement can be seen. A spark of color may be needed to set the spirit of the piece. Other times, a change to fill the configuration can be made so that all looks right to your eye—perhaps something must be added, subtracted, or moved. Vary the layout and let the quilt speak to you. You will feel—know—when it is finally correct.

When you are satisfied with your design, make a sketch or take a snapshot of it for reference, but remember that this arrangement isn't set in stone. You may feel the inspiration to change and add components as you go along, This is fine; let it happen and consider the changes to be the suggestions of the wise spirits that watch over creative matters.

Also keep in mind that when you are finished with the complete assembly and quilting process, the quilt will look somewhat different from your first impression. The size and texture of the piece will be changed by the process of sewing and handling, the binding together of layers by the pattern stitching called quilting. It will also lose some of its dimension because of fabric turned under for seams.

How and When Do I Add the Calligraphy?

Add ideograms before cloth is sewn to the body of the quilt.

In Chapter Three, Chinese characters for twenty key words are given for your use. Through the passage of thousands of years, the beautifully formed ideograms stand for more than a thought or a single word. Each brush-stroked symbol derives from centuries of artistic practice, beginning in the very mists of time when priests interpreted cracks in shell and bone as a form of divination for kings. The study of the characters is still considered a means of spiritual elevation, a matter of letting the "true spirit within flow free . . . ."

Select the Chinese ideograms that express what you are longing for. For a love quilt, I included ideograms for harmony, happiness, love, and patience—qualities I feel are important for a successful relationship.

Several methods may be used to add the ideograms. There is a simple iron-on appliqué technique, or the ideograms may be drawn with permanent black laundry pen on cloth, painted with fabric paint, or brush stroked with diluted bleach onto dark fabric. Whatever process you select, test the method first on an extra scrap of the cloth you'll be using. And, after you have placed the final markings on your fabric, allow the piece of fabric to dry completely for several hours or overnight before putting the ink, paint, or bleach into contact with other components of the quilt.

I have found it useful to photocopy the character, sometimes enlarging the ideogram slightly. I use two copies—I cut up one to physically place the strokes and the second as reference for proper positioning of my strokes. When using the cloth iron-on appliqué technique the characters are more easily handled if they are fairly large. If you intend to paint, stencil, or trace the ideogram, the character may be smaller. Make a test piece if you are in doubt. Take your time with this step.

If you choose to use an appliqué or fabric bonding method, use a fabric bonding film such as Wonderunder, which is a paper backed heat-activated thin dry glue tissue used for cloth. Wonderunder is inexpensive, simple to use, and can be purchased at fabric stores, craft outlets, or stores like Wal-Mart. Read the instructions that come with the bonding film before using it!

Bond black fabric to a square of bonding film. Using the paper copy of the ideogram as a pattern, either mark around the paper or pin the pieces to the bonded cloth, then cut. Again, making a test piece is a good idea to perfect your technique.

Carefully arrange the ideogram strokes where you want them—once they are ironed on, they cannot be moved. Refer to the original ideogram in Chapter Three or to your reference copy and place the cutouts on the cloth. Leave at least an inch of fabric from the cut edge to the spot you are applying the ideogram as a seam allowance.

After bonding the ideogram to your work, you may wish to add several lines of machine or hand stitching over the black fabric. The thread enhances the appearance of brush strokes, but it is a strictly aesthetic convention that I prefer for my quilts.

If you prefer not to use an appliqué or fabric bonding process, brush strokes can also be cut out of cloth and hot glued or fabric glued to the quilt without the use of bonding film.

You may also choose to paint the ideograms directly onto your fabric with fabric paint or black laundry marker. If you prefer to paint them, please practice the ideogram several times on paper and scraps of cloth before attempting the final product on the body of the quilt. Each time you make a brush or pen stroke, think of the virtue represented by this character. There may be several you wish to include—some examples are energy, courage, vigor, spirit, or tranquility.

I placed the ideogram for harmony over the pocket area of a shirt I used in a love quilt. Amulets and notes can be placed under the ideogram in the pocket.

Motifs from fabric prints may also be cut out and heat-bonded as described. For example, if you want a picture of a lion or pansy, find fabric with this print. Iron on the backing, cut out the motif. Peel off the backing and iron the design where you wish. It is not necessary to stitch around or over the added design.

My Cloth Is Charged, I've Gathered My Embellishments and Inclusions, I've Done My Starting Rituals. Now What?

In this section, the general method of construction for any of the magic wish quilts is detailed.

The actual construction is begun from the center, then you will work your way out to the edges. Spread out your pinned cloth with the batting side up. Lay the fabric that is to be in the center of the quilt on the prepared batting and backing "sandwich," right side up, flat on the batting. Remove any safety pins that are under the patch (see page 26).

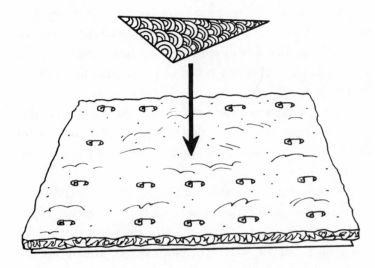

Once you have prepared your batting and backing, place the first panel of your construction at the center of the batting.

At this point, place any herbs, written wishes or amulets you want under this central panel on the batting, under the cloth. Pat the area gently and the batting should hold the things in place. Pin the edges of the fabric with straight pins. Avoid putting herbs or hidden charms in the actual seam allowance—where one piece of fabric joins another—as it will be difficult, if not impossible, to sew through them.

You will notice that some inclusions will be too lumpy if hidden between layers; you may wish to put these in small pockets, or affix them to the surface of the fabric. But if you prefer to tuck these objects inside the quilt, be assured that a quilt that is a little bumpy is fine—this type of quilt is not going to be perfectly flat.

If the object is something that might crumble easily but is too large to put between layers, such as a flower, the item may be placed inside an envelope made of cloth or inside a pocket. Avoid any plastic bags or wraps—a slightly moist item such as a leaf or flower will continue to desiccate if enclosed in fabric or paper, but will retain moisture and rot if wrapped or sealed in plastic.

Pockets can be any size and will act like envelopes to hold precious notes and mementos. A rectangular piece of fabric may be folded just like an envelope: dampen a paper envelope so that the glue loosens and carefully unfold the paper. Use the paper as your pattern to cut a piece of fabric to the proper shape. After you've cut the piece of fabric, fold the cloth in the same manner as the paper and press the shape with your iron to keep the folds intact. Where the paper uses glue, you stitch or use a hot glue gun. Be sure to leave the flap open so you can insert your written wishes. You may wish to make several of these simple pocket-envelopes in different sizes and sew them to the quilt. You may even want to "address" them using a fine-tip fabric marker pen. A button, snap, decorative pin, or ribbon tie can be added so that the flap may be closed and opened at will. These pockets should be added after the construction of the top of the quilt is completed.

Handle the pinned quilt carefully to avoid dislodging the hidden items. Machine sew or hand sew all the way around all edges of the pinned-on patch, ¼ to ½ inch in from the edge of the added cloth, through all layers of fabric, batting and backing (see diagram below). You will be able to see the stitches on the back. For a sewing machine stitch size, use 6 to 8 stitches per inch. Small stitches will make the seam pucker; large stitches have elasticity. The raw edges of this first piece will be covered with the addition of the other panels of cloth.

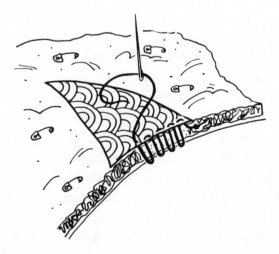

After you have placed your inclusions and are ready to affix the panel to the batting and backing, this cross-sectional view shows how to sew through the layers.

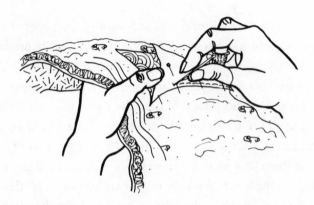

Lay the next panel face down on the previous panel. Pin the edges along the seam you wish to sew. Then stitch along this edge to attach the new panel.

The next patch of fabric will be laid face to face against the first central beginning piece and sewn on one side, then flipped back to be right side up. Try this method to test the position of the second cloth by pinning along the side you will sew. Flip the patch over and see if the position is what you had anticipated before sewing it into place.

Pin with straight pins at the edges of the first piece and this second piece. Sew this one seam through all layers: patches, batting and backing. Remove the pins.

Flip the new piece out so that the cloth lies right side up, flat and smooth. Do not iron; instead pat the fabric flat with your hand and check that you are satisfied with the placement. Flip back the patch and remove any safety pins under piece number two, add any secret items to be concealed under this new panel as you did with the central piece.

Continue to add patches or strips around the perimeter of the center piece with this method until a satisfactory size is achieved. Varying lengths and widths of the cloth strips and pieces create visual interest—you can even add different straight-sided shapes by placing the fabric diagonally across a corner rather than square with the edge. Continue in this fashion until you have added the borders in the same fashion and the entire batting and backing is covered.

This process may take several days to achieve to your satisfaction. Don't forget to place the secret herbs, stones, notes, and other items you have selected behind the patches before you sew them down. When the cover is done, add the pockets. Do not rush through any of these steps. Take time to meditate over the purpose in the composition of this artistic talisman.

This Looks Good But It's Not a Quilt Yet. Now What?

At this point, stitching patterns should be drawn on the quilt in chalk or soap. I use a narrow sliver of scented soap—sandalwood is my personal favorite. Don't use pencil, ballpoint, or marking pen—they are permanent and you won't be able to see your stitches properly. Remember that a magic talisman quilt cannot, and should not, be washed.

Pattern stitching, the actual "quilting," should be done by hand. Although the stitches do not have to be small, they should be as even as possible. They are important symbols of the binding of your intent to this purpose. The stitching represents knot magic, the theme of uniting and binding an intent and quality to the object.

Knots were believed to restrain mischievous demons and a properly tied knot could cast a spell to hold a lover. At one time, knots were tied in garments to ward off calamity. A popular Southern superstition (derived from a practice of the Cherokee) was to tie a tight knot in the corner of a sheet if an owl was heard. The twist would tie up the tongue of death, represented by this night bird.

Knots and braids are of deep significance in the Orient. In Buddhism, the mystic knot is one of the eight spiritual treasures, symbolizing never-ending vigilance, watchfulness, eternal wisdom and the duration of spiritual life. The endless knot *p'an-chang* is called the "knot of happiness."

The even stitches of the Japanese *sashiko* technique of stitching are perfect for this use. Sashiko uses a thick cotton thread (pearl size); a larger needle than the traditional American quilting needle; and simple, even, well-defined stitches in patterns that are representative of nature. The thicker cotton thread is strong and easy to handle and the needle has a large, easy-to-thread eye. A frame or hoop is not necessary.

Sashiko uses a simple, in-and-out sewing stitch, often called the running stitch (see Chapter One, page 4). Currently,

Stitching represents knot magic—uniting and binding an intent and quality to the object.

American quilting is adapting this technique and calling it "large stitch" or "easy stitch" quilting. Even if you do not use a traditional sashiko pattern, the method of thick thread, large-eyed needle, no quilting frame, and large, even stitches is one quickly mastered by a beginner. Simply sketch your design on the fabric with soap or chalk and follow the lines with your needle. Do not use pencil or pen—the marks will show after you've finished stitching.

Use pearl cotton thread, embroidery floss, or a double strand of regular quilting thread. Don't forget to use a thimble to protect your finger and to make penetration of the fabric easier. The thimble is usually placed on the middle finger of the stitching hand—take a few test stitches to determine your pushing finger, that's the one that should wear the thimble.

If an area is hard to "needle" because of something hidden inside, stick the needle in and gently wiggle the point to move the object aside slightly. In the case of most leaves, flowers, herbs, and even paper, it is possible to simply jab through the item.

There are many traditional sashiko patterns, each with a message sewn into the threads. The design of overlapping circles, referred to as *shippo* or "seven treasures or linked gems," is reminiscent of the American quilt pattern "Double Wedding Ring." The interlocked rings symbolize unity and the joining of two lives when used on a quilt planned for love or harmony. The overlapped rings of shippo also represent Oriental treasures of linked gems. If you wish to use the shippo pattern, you can simply trace around a teacup or saucer to make the layout of interlocking rings.

The sashiko pattern of "blue waves" is a graphically simple repetition of lapping arcs, similar to fish scales. Blue waves may also be reproduced with the help of a teacup and chalk. Blue waves can bring the symbolic power of the element of water to your work. Geometric octagons are the sashiko image of turtle shells, wishing for long life and health.

Inventing your own patterns adds personal meaning and power to your work. If you are not sure of how your graphic idea will work out, try the pattern out on a scrap of cloth first. Stitching words and names in the border of the quilt is also artistically and magically effective. Make quilting based on words simple by eliminating flourishes; go for a large, clean, flowing style that is simple to follow with needle and thread. Keep your design and stitches large and loose—each letter should be at least an inch in height. Writing in thread can be done by hand stitching or with your sewing machine. I have used this script method using my old sewing machine with the feed dogs covered; consult your sewing machine manual for "freestyle embroidery" or "darning" methods.

Always include a tracing of your (the maker's) hand somewhere on the work—if not in the pattern stitching, then as a painted or drawn sketch or appliqué—on the front or the back of the quilt. The hand is the part of the human body appearing most frequently as a magical symbol throughout the ages—recall the power of the prehistoric handprints in the painted caves of France.

The hand has been a magical symbol throughout the ages...add your handprint to your quilts.

Contact with the hand can represent "the magic touch," and the "laying on of hands" can confer a blessing or healing. A hand can be the symbol of friendly acceptance (a handshake), an indication of prayer (folded hands), unity and strength (a fist), loyalty (clasped hands), or giving of a promise or oath (raised hand).

What Is Embellishment?

In the art of quilting, the attachment of small decorations—such as beads, jewelry, or ribbons—to the surface of the quilt is called embellishment.

After you've completed the pattern stitching, amulets may be sewn, tied, or hot glued on the surface of the quilt. One simple way to do this is to fasten a length of narrow ribbon at the midpoint of the ribbon to the body of the quilt, then tie on the amulet. This act will also bring the force of knot magic to the amulet's power.

Amulets on a love quilt I made for a friend included a ribbon from a special gift box of chocolate, crystal points dug during a personal expedition, a silver Lady Kuan Yin pendant, a favorite earring, a small silver dragon for wisdom and protection, a handpainted cloth Valentine given as a gift to the bride, lace from her wedding dress, and a propitious fortune cookie paper. Shiny beads, a small mirror, and gold cloth were added for the symbolic deflection of envy and negative thoughts. Tiny books (representing the bride's profession as a writer), coins (the groom is an accountant), and jewels (to represent abundance and wealth) are scattered about in a wish for prosperity and success. Wishes and blessings may be written on the fabric surface (front and back) with permanent marking pens or fabric markers. Such messages are also hidden within the layers of fabric.

But Wait...the Edges Aren't Finished. And How Can I Hang Up My Quilt?

To complete the quilt, edges should be bound with cotton quilt binding or with a strip of fabric in the chosen color or protective pattern.

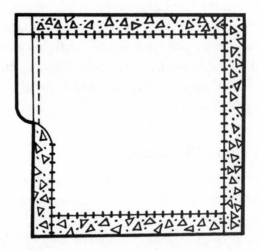

This shows a simple binding. A strip of cloth is sewn to the edges of the quilt on the front, then turned over to the back and stitched to cover the raw edges.

It is possible to add a second backing, sewing around three and a half sides, pillowcase fashion (page 33, top). Turn the work inside out and whip shut the open space. Binding is not needed in this method. This leaves a clean edge and back finish, and any pattern stitching you've done will not be seen from the back (page 33, bottom).

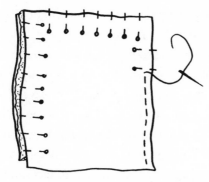

To make a pillowcase-type backing, first take your backing material and attach it on three sides to your construction. Backing fabric
should be face to face with the front of the quilt.

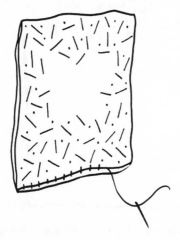

After attaching the backing, turn the work right side out and whip
shut the open space.

Instead of binding, a second backing may be added before
doing the actual quilting. The pillowcase method is followed
as described above. After the work is turned, you can then do
the quilting.

This method can be desirable because any stitching motifs
can be seen on the reverse of the quilt, but incidental stitching that fastened on the patches or embellishments, which
can make the back of the quilt look fairly messy, is covered.
However, the additional thickness of the cloth can make
quilting more difficult, and stitches will of necessity be
larger. This method eliminates the need to bind the edges.
The "pillowcase backing" technique is a very neat finish and

aesthetically worthwhile if the quilt will be kept loose rather than fixed to a wall or hidden away.

If you do not wish to hang the quilt, you are now finished, and your special wish talisman quilt is ready for your use.

If the quilt is to be hung, there are several methods that may be used. Cloth or ribbon loops can be added at the top. Loops may be stitched or caught on decorative hangers, in the fashion of a shower curtain (see diagram below). Small cafe-curtain rings may also be used to facilitate hanging.

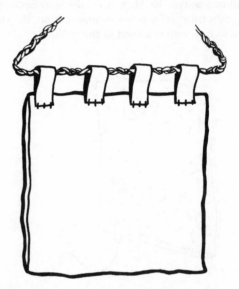

To hang your talisman on a decorative hanger, one option is to attach loops to the back of the fabric.

A sleeve, the width of the quilt, may be sewn on to the back of the quilt, and a dowel inserted (see page 35). Leave several inches of the dowel sticking out on each end of the sleeve. Use hooks or hangers to suspend the quilt this way. I have seen very beautiful hangers in the form of brass stars, cut crystal knobs, and fanciful animals that would enhance the beauty of your work.

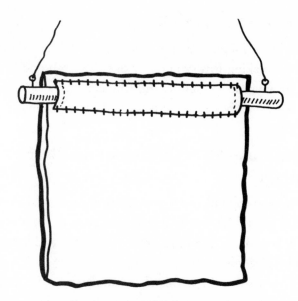

You can attach a sleeve to the back of your talisman and insert a dowel as a hanging option.

It's Beautiful, but Something Is Missing. What Should I Add?

Before you perform your closing ritual, a final sensory dimension may be added to your work. Fragrances in the forms of incense, candles, and perfumes are among the oldest methods of gaining the attention of the spirits and forces we cannot see. As the scent rises from a magically charged incense, the powers within the herbs and spices are released to attract or repel these spirits or forces as we have placed the intent within them.

Fragrances create an aura of attraction. Think of the mystery and magnetism of a perfumed love letter bearing a fragile promise in the elusive scent that awakens memory. Essential oils can be stroked lightly on the fabric of your beautiful handmade product; dab the fragrances on the back of the quilt in case the oil base leaves a stain. Many essential oils sold are synthetic; the real thing is usually very expensive. Synthetic oils are adequate for use here; the intent is what is important. The aroma should please you and remind you of your goal in making this quilt.

I've Finished . . . or Have I?

Lay your beautiful talisman out before you. Meditate on your purpose in making this symbol. Stroke the cloth gently and notice the mysterious bumps and tiny crackly noises where your powerful wishes and desires are hidden in the folds.

How do I use My Talisman to the Best Advantage?

Will you hang the quilt so that you can see the bold banner while you work? Or will you fold the creation carefully in the work box, nestled in tissue, to be taken out and caressed as you visualize your desires?

You may wish to drape this cloth amulet over the foot of your bed, to draw over your body as your dream. The assembly of so many pieces and parts, scents and stones are all to be used as an aid to let you unlock the potential within your spirit.

In the following chapters, which will detail suggestions for magic quilts for several different purposes, a closing ritual will be provided. But the most meaningful ritual is one that you devise, one that will give you a feeling of freeing the power of your dormant energies to achieve what you need.

From time to time, after you have finished your talisman, it is good to recharge the magic by exposing the work to the light of the Moon on a solstice. This is especially necessary if you feel the charm has been working heavily toward the fruition of your wishes. If the charm had been exposed to bad influences, such as discord between emotional partners or severe disorder or contention in the immediate physical surroundings, airing the talisman in the strong, unshaded light of the full Moon or in the fiery cleansing of the noon Sun may erase any malignant lingering influences that try to cling to it.

Chapter 3

Calligraphy

Ephemeral Beauty of Thought Captured in Ink

I ro ha

Though gay in hue, the blossoms flutter down, alas!
Who then, in this world of ours, may continue
* forever?*
Crossing today the uttermost limits of
* phenomenal existence,*
I shall see no more fleeting dreams, neither be
* any longer intoxicated.*

—Kukai (774–835)

Calligraphy means "words written by hand." Characters convey the language of thought, the artistic beauty of that thought, words and concepts linked in the flowing brush strokes of night-dark ink. The characters reflect an ancient history of humanity and the values and ideas that drive the interior forces of individuals within society. The brush is guided by the spirit of the heart, the flow of the inner self.

The overall impression of the calligraphic stroke has the power to convey sentiments, mood, ideas, nuances of thought and movement. It is more than an idea. The essence and vitality of the element of nature expressed in the ink strokes contains the *ch'i*, the life energy, of the thing itself. There is little doubt that the flowing silk of calligraphic brushstrokes contain magic within them. By the inscription of a word-thought, an abstract painting of depth and substance may appear in the viewer's mind.

Dim history records the original impulse to the art of calligraphy as inspired in 2700 B.C. by footprints of birds and animals. There are precious examples of oracle bone and turtle shell inscriptions dated as early as 1766 B.C. These markings were regarded as a manifestation of the power of nature, the will of heaven written for human's instruction.

The lines of calligraphy ink should be as solid and strong as bone to convey the vital tension of life into the ideographic character. To practice the art of calligraphy, seven basic strokes must be mastered. They are known as the seven mysteries. When all seven strokes are mastered, the first ideogram that can be formed, using all seven strokes, is the mystic pictogram for *eternity*. There are many schools of calligraphic style. Their names reflect the individual artistic custom of the founder of the school and conventions of their practice: Mad Grass, Shell and Bone, Stone-Drum, Bell and Pot, The Three Perfections, Clerical, Cursive, and Block.

While living in Japan, I saw in homes, temples, and places of business, calligraphic characters carefully framed and displayed in places seen frequently in daily activities. The character represented a cluster of associations, qualities, and aspirations. If the word *prosperity* was printed there, the meaning encompassed not only today's groceries, but the ability to provide for one's descendants in the future. The word meant to work with the hands, but also to shape one's thoughts, to plan materially and mentally in a way that would aim every effort and chance event toward a beneficial end. The character reminded the viewer to focus on a goal, and by focusing, to activate the powers both human and supernatural to bring about a change.

I was struck by the effect such a device could produce. This is why I emphasize the use of calligraphy on these magic quilts.

Important Characters for Use

Some of the thoughts will be represented by two or three ideograms. Each is made up of several elements that enhance the concept illustrated. You may use one, several, or all of the characters.

These calligraphic characters were drawn by a dear friend who is the daughter of a traditional heritage of artists and the wife of a man who represents generations of Zen scholars.

Ho. The ideogram for *harmony*. Everything in proper proportions; moderation of desires achieving inner harmony; that time when all creatures are properly nourished.

An. The ideogram for *tranquility*. Things in the proper place; all things in order; universal energies in harmony.

Ai. The ideogram for *love*. An inspiration of breath that brings life to the heart and bodily grace. The supreme emotion.

Jen. The ideogram for *patience*. A firm heart, one that has patience and tolerance.

Mei. The ideogram for *beauty*. Docility and tranquility; absence of resistance.

Fu. The ideogram for *happiness*. Happiness comes from the inner life, not material things; an existence untroubled by hunger in any way.

Sun. The ideogram for *gentleness*. A leaf in a stream, borne by water without exerting will or resistance.

Shih. The ideogram for *honesty*. Ten thousand coins under a roof; fortune denotes superiority of character, therefore honesty.

Ch'i. The ideogram for *energy*. Spiritual energy, the universal breath that gives us material existence. Literal translation is "breath" or "vitality." The essence, destiny, talent, moving force of our singular life.

Ying. The ideogram for *courage*. No fear in an open place; the heroic one shows courage, conquering hardship by harmonizing with nature.

Shih. The ideogram for *revelation*. Manifestation of a heaven-sent omen; the secret is revealed; discovery; the opening of knowledge.

Kuei. The ideogram for *honor*. A basket of cash; expensive reward; an inner quality more precious than jade yet concealed.

P'ing. The ideogram for *peace*. The balance between opposing forces; bamboo stem balanced by a tongue of fire; equal shields on either side leads to peace.

Shu. The ideogram for *forgiveness*. The natural benevolence of the heart is to forgive.

Chih. The ideogram for *wisdom*. A combination of the strokes for "oath," "spoken," "knowledge," and "sun." Knowledge that spreads to benefit and enlighten.

Shen. The ideogram for *spirit*. The inner spirit of our life; character combined with other characters produces terms related to our inner condition as it manifested in our life.

Chien. The ideogram for *vigor*. A complex character hinting of the means to power through knowledge.

Ming. The ideogram for *enlightenment*. The thought that all things are one. Formed by combination of the strokes for "Sun" and "Moon."

Hsin. The ideogram for *devotion*. The implication of trust; to abandon doubts; devotion inspired by honesty.

Chi Shi Ki. The ideogram for *knowledge*. Enlightenment; to perceive truth; scope of information; the capacity of sound judgment; depth and ripeness of experience; the quest that has come to fruition.

The *hanko*, or signature seal of the artist of these characters (seal is enlarged). The seal itself is hand carved in a special chosen stone. The characters are those of ancient Chinese, almost archaic usage. The talented artist's name is Nakaseko Tamami, but her art-name depicted in the seal lettering is Jusen.

Chapter 4

The Use of Candles

Flame, Vehicle, and Element of Transformation

*Your hearts know in silence the secrets of the days
and the nights. But your ears thirst for the sound
of your heart's knowledge.*

—Kalil Gibran

Burning candles to produce or enhance a mood is common. Light and fire symbolize the life-giving properties of the Sun. To our "old lizard brain"—the most primitive part of the brain holding our ancestral memories and most basic instincts—the small flame gives the comfort and reassurance that a blazing torch or bonfire in the cave once provided. The mastery of spark and flame gives us a feeling of power and assures us of our mindful control over the elements of the unseen. Not so harmless as simply flipping a switch to light the room, a candle—a miniature torch—must be tended and respected.

Fire, or the representative of fire, a candle, has been a requirement of working magic since time out of mind. A blaze protects and defends, illuminates and alchemizes. Flame is the vehicle and element of transformation. Perhaps from our atavistic remembrances of caves, forests, castle halls, and cottages, candlelight creates an ambiance of intimacy and safety, even a feeling of sexuality. Certainly candle glow is kinder and easier on the eyes than incandescent or fluorescent lighting.

Altars of all faiths support candles. Teachings of the Christian church are often expressed symbolically according to numbers, color, and position: six tapers on the altar represent the constant round of prayer within the church, three candles signify the presence of the Trinity. Tapers, torches, and small flames were frequently used in Renaissance art to portray religious meanings. The use of candles at shrines and in processions is universal and can be observed in holy places of all faiths.

Ancient altar pieces wrought to support sacred tapers are precious treasures. For your own uses, be certain your candle holders are sturdy and safe. Beauty is a consideration, but in handling one of Nature's powerful elements, use caution and respect. Crystal holders add sparkle and beauty, and are generally heavy enough to safely support a long-burning taper. Crystal or glass holders will crack, however, if left unattended with a low flame. Holders made of copper increase the affinity with the element of earth, while handmade ceramic candelabra are earthy and intimate, especially if you have made them yourself.

Small, enclosed votive light holders are the safest containers for small candles. The walls of the votive cup are high to protect the flame from drafts and spills. You may wish to use a *bobech*, drip shield, to ensure against wax running down tall tapers. Don't use plastic or wooden holders as there can be a fire hazard from these combustible materials. Never place an open flame near curtains or hangings, dried flowers, loose paper, or where a child or pet could knock the taper over.

Select a candle color by determining the tint that will aid in your endeavor. For example, use light blue to increase tranquility and improve health. Red draws physical vigor and strength, and adds passion and protection to those in the home. White gives protection, increases sincerity, and strengthens truth. Black defends against evil and deflects negative thoughts—both those directed against you and your own feelings of negativity. Green brings luck, prosperity, and increased vibrations for healing.

Use a light blue candle to increase feelings of tranquility and to improve health.

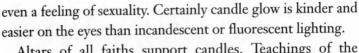

Often three or more candles are used: a color honoring the
day or season, a singularly colored and dressed candle indicating wishful intent, and a white taper to enhance the spirituality of purpose. The lists below may be used for selection of
colors for candles and for cloth for your quilt. This compila-
tion of color usage is adapted from *Practical Candleburning
Rituals* by Raymond Buckland, and *Earth, Air, Fire and Water*
by Scott Cunningham, both from Llewellyn Publications.

Symbolism of Colors

Black is the absence of color and casts away or negates
nastiness, hostility, and baneful thoughts directed
toward us. Black protects against illness, enhances
concentration, shores up resolve, gives protection,
averts evil, ameliorates loss, mediates discord, brings
about harmony from confusion, and neutralizes
negative thoughts.

Blue, dark curbs impulsiveness, lifts depression, stabilizes
changeability, aids meditation and the spirit of peace.

Blue, light signifies the element of water. This shade
brings tranquility, increasing understanding, patience,
focus of good health, healthful sleep, aura of twilight,
devotion, happiness, and serenity—it is the color of
philosophy. Skyblue is the traditional color of the Virgin Mary and indicates heavenly love.

Brown candles can be burned to lift blocks of hesitation
or uncertainty. It also aids neutrality and is useful in
working animal magic.

Gold or yellow increases attraction, smoothes persua-
sion, bolsters charm and confidence, intellect, and
healthful stimulation of the mind. It gives energy,
charisma, communication, and happiness. Yellow is the
element Air and the color of science, the Sun, and
divinity. Gold and yellow are also symbolic of revealed
truth and the color of Chinese royalty.

Green is the color of the element of earth and nature and
is the Druidic color of knowledge. It aids finance, fertility, good luck, profitable employment, material

growth, beneficial medicine, comfort, and resilience. Green symbolizes the triumph of spring over winter, and life over death. Green suggests charity and regeneration of the soul through good works.

Greenish yellow acts to psychically banish sickness, erase cowardice, turn away anger, cure jealousy, and soothe discord.

Pink attracts honor, love, morality, and weddings. It promotes emotional union, repairs damaged self-esteem, and increases compassion. Pink also aids expression of music and stimulates emotions of well-being and happiness.

Purple eases tension, aids ambition and business progress, brings personal power and enhancement of spiritual activities, indicates religion, speeds healing of severe diseases or problems, and acts as a psychic power amplifier. This is the color of Western royalty and, by association, the color of the Christian God the Father.

Silver and gray symbolize encouragement, aid adaptability, stimulate stale and unused personal talents; and give powers of attraction, conciliation, and charm.

Red is the element of fire—energy, bodily strength, health, vigor, sexual love, passion, and defensive magic. Red is the color of blood, which is associated with the emotions, thus a tint of both love and hate. In Oriental thought, it is the color of happiness and prosperity. Scarlet was the color of sovereign power among the ancient Romans.

White is associated with the Moon and with qualities of purity, truth, sincerity, and protection. In Christian iconography, white is symbolic of innocence of soul, purity, and holiness of life. The Roman vestal virgins wore white, a practice said to lead to the custom of white bridal dresses. If you can't find the color you want, white is all-purpose when used with strong visualization and works for all positive purposes.

Colors Associated with Days of the Week

Sunday: yellow

Monday: white

Tuesday: red

Wednesday: purple

Thursday: blue

Friday: green

Saturday: black

Beeswax candles are traditional for altar use as they are thought to be pure, and thus more suitable for use in the area of divinity. Beeswax is closely associated with nature and burns with a clear hot flame, without drips, soot, or smoke. Candles of animal fat, or tallow, are considered unclean. Beeswax tapers are the most expensive candle produced, so many times clean burning candles made of vegetable or mineral (paraffin) products are used.

Never use a melted, blemished, or cracked candle unless the disfigurement can be used to enhance your magic in some way. A broken candle heals itself as the heat and flame passes down the wax; the break fuses, heals and then disappears. This type of imagery is helpful for such purposes as producing harmony after a dispute or creating physical wholeness after an illness.

Many people do not use a taper that has been used for some other purpose. Some feel that the candle has been infused with power for a definite objective and using the taper again would be a haphazard use of energy. As Scott Cunningham states firmly, "One spell to a candle."

To use your candles most effectively for your wish magic, it is necessary to know the general process for dressing or charging the candle. Hold the individual candle between both palms and press gently while picturing as clearly as possible the fruition of your desire. State your purpose. See the completion of your wish. Breathe deeply and imagine pushing power and energy into the candle. Then, using a sharp point, carefully inscribe into the candle wax an emblem of the request. The inscription could be just a word or two, or perhaps a symbol such as a rune that represents the wish. This helps to focus your thoughts. When inscribing, don't press too hard or the wax may crack through or crumble. For candle magic involving love spells, a rose thorn is often suggested for use as an inscribing tool.

Next, choose the proper scented oil for your purpose. Start at the center of the candle and rub to the top while concentrating on or saying out loud an invocation of your wish. Stroke all around the wax (or five strokes), from middle to the wick end. Repeat this step, rubbing from center to bottom. If aromatic essential oil is not available, use a combination of olive or vegetable (not animal) oil and a few drops of honey. Use sparingly as the additional oil will often make the flame spatter or spark. Place candle firmly and evenly upright in a holder.

If you are using more than one candle, use a fresh match to light each taper.

A glass or crystal hurricane shield or lamp glass is useful for protecting the flame and allowing a taper to burn out totally. If a candle is shielded in such a way, the taper will burn slowly, evenly, and in a safe manner. In order to let a candle burn completely, it may be necessary to set the holder in your bathtub or fireplace, or place the candle and holder in a large metal pot or cauldron so that the hot wax and flame is protected from accident. Allow the candle to burn out completely; do not blow it out. By pinching out the flame, you are locking or stopping the energy you desire to release.

If it is absolutely necessary to extinguish your candle, carefully walk outside with the taper and let the natural breeze take away the flame. It is also proper to use a clean silver knife blade to snuff the light, but do not reuse the candle for magic if the flame must be interrupted in this way.

Candle magic is probably the most common folk magic practiced in all cultures. Do not use it for frivolous yearnings and petty gain. Respect the power of candle magic and use it thoughtfully.

Chapter 5

When to Begin a Project

Full Moons and Days of the Week

*What nature delivers to us is never stale. Because
what nature creates has eternity in it.*

—Isaac Bashevis Singer

Success in life's endeavors can often be aided by choosing the right time to begin. One would not plant petunias in November . . . common sense says this effort would be doomed from the start. Yet we often fail to consider such elementary forces when we embark on much bigger and bolder projects.

The day selected for launching your wish to the attention of the Universe will have a significant effect upon the strength of the charm. For example, beginning a talisman for prosperity in business on a Sunday in the Mead Moon of July would sharpen the effectiveness of the project. Every date, color, image, object, and fragrance helps refine and enhance the power of your talisman. Choose a date after thoughtful reflection. The sages of olden days spent much of their deliberations calculating auspicious dates for royal endeavors. In many countries, important moves such as setting a wedding date, beginning building construction, making business mergers, having medical operations or

producing a major family or business decision are not com-
menced without intense scrutiny for a cosmically correct
"birth date."

The information on the following pages is adapted from
Reclaiming the Power by Lady Sabrina (Llewellyn, 1992).

The Full Moons

Selecting a date begins with picking an auspicious month
for commencement. Each month in its turn has potency to
add to your cause. This list begins with November, the
beginning of the Wiccan new year.

> **November** is the month of the Snow Moon. It indicates
> the death of the old year and beginning of the new. It is
> a time of the underworld and darkness. It is a time to
> get rid of bad vibrations, negative thoughts and energies.

> **December** is the month of the Oak Moon. Deep winter
> calls for the steadfastness of the great oak. The shape
> of reality is obscured by cold and dark. Remain stead-
> fast in your principles. Your candle will be lit by faith
> of things not seen.

> **January** is the month of the Wolf Moon. The Lord of Life
> has been reborn. Hope is kindled. The wolf protects in
> the snow. Consider new options and prospects; protect
> what you have. It is a time of optimistic conservation.

> **February** is the month of the Storm Moon. Darkness
> and cold will soon be ended. It is a time to plan for the
> future and to anticipate new endeavors. Ice begins to
> melt, the river stretches.

> **March** is the month of the Chaste Moon. It is the end
> of winter and uncertainty; the Goddess returns full
> of promise. Seeds may be planted with certainty of
> fruition. The rivers run strong.

> **April** is the month of the Seed Moon. The sap rises in
> the forest; leaves open. Green spring, growth and
> desire. The herd increases. Smell the brown earth.
> Time to plant spiritual and physical seeds; put wishes
> into motion.

May is the month of the Hare Moon. Flowers cascade and the air is fragrant. It is full springtime—time of the fruitful hare gamboling in the meadow. Life blossoms into creativity. Set and attain goals.

June is the month of the Dyad Moon. It is a period to seek balance between opposites under the influences of the Heavenly Twins, Castor and Pollux. Endeavor to achieve union, set forces and matters right, make peace between spiritual and physical desires.

July is the month of the Mead Moon—a month of warmth, abundance, and fat in the land. It is a time of fullness of crops; plan for preservation and future use of the fruits of this year's work. Contemplation in the hot Sun. What is to be done when your goals are reached?

August is the month of the Wort Moon—a Moon of golden wheat. It is first harvest-time; sharpen the scythe. Begin to reap and plan to utilize and preserve what you have attained.

September is the month of the Barley Moon. It is the Great Harvest; the virgin carries sheaves of grain—a time for celebration and realization that goals have been reached. Yet it is a time to spin, knit, preserve, and prepare for the coming cold.

October is the month of the Blood Moon. Red wine and fresh meat is offered in thanksgiving to the deities for what we have attained in this year's turn of the wheel of seasons. Time for hunting. Blood flows to continue the force of life in the coming darkness. Prepare for the cold. Remember the ones who have passed.

The Days of the Week

The seven days of the week have natural, magical correspondences to special astrological energies that may enhance the attainment of a goal. Strength and energy are added to our endeavors when they are enacted on the proper day.

Sunday is the day of the Sun. A powerful time good for creative, positive and spiritual works. Things may be activated that are related to patronage for business, acquiring money, health, and friendship. A day of high masculine energy.

element: fire
colors: shades of gold and yellow
metal and gems: gold, diamond, topaz, tiger's eye.

Monday is the day of the Moon—a day for introspective, inner-directed energies. Make up your week's plans today; schedule your meditation times. Power is focused on matters concerning development of self-expression, inspiration, enhancement of psychic ability, changes. Monday will add power to a work to build inner harmony. A day of feminine energy; day of the Goddess.

element: water
colors: silver or white
metal and gems: silver, pearl, clear quartz, moonstone

Tuesday is the day of Mars. Power! Energy! Things are moving! A day for developing courage, physical strength, protection of property and investments. A good day for the gym, but don't start arguments. A warlike, masculine day. Mars' day can be the time to start a protection or energy talisman quilt.

element: fire
color: red, red, red
metals and gems: iron, bloodstone, ruby, garnet

Wednesday is the day of Mercury. This is the day I get most of my writing done. Could it be because Wednesday is the day for communication? Mercury influences business deals and getting your ideas into the open air, a day for career advancement. The day of Mercury's influence may be the day to begin a talisman for harmony in your life if you think communication is a problem influencing that area. Healing is another of Mercury's talents, so think of Wednesday for beginning a healing work.

element: air
color: energetic, look-at-me yellow
metals and gems: quicksilver, opal, agate, adventurine

Thursday is the day of Jupiter. Jupiter is big, big, big and this planet influences expansion, ambition, and idealism. Legal and career success as well as situations concerning money should be nudged along with the help of Jupiter. Jupiter can help express religious expansion.

> **element:** water
> **color:** deep blue or spiritual dark purple
> **metals and gems:** tin, amethyst, lepidolote, lapis

Friday is the day of Venus. Sex and sensuality are under the rule of beautiful, bright Venus. It's definitely the day to start work on that love talisman. Love and attraction, good relationships and union between opposites are all in the air on Friday.

> **element:** earth or water
> **color:** the color of the life-force—green
> **metals and gems:** copper, rose quartz, emerald, chrysocolla

Saturday is the day of Saturn. Saturn owns the karmic law of limitation. The principle of learning through trial and error and the ability to discipline ourselves is activated most strongly on Saturday. If your projects tend to get grandiose, then trail off and remain unfinished, perhaps the influence of Saturn is needed.

> **element:** earth
> **color:** black
> **gems:** onyx, obsidian, jet

Chapter 6

A Quilt to Bring Love

A Talisman of Affection and Amour

My heart is like a singing bird
Whose nest is in a watered shoot;
My heart is like an apple tree
Whose boughs are bent with thickset fruit;
My heart is like a rainbow shell
That paddles in a halcyon sea;
My heart is gladder than all these
Because my love is come to me.

—Christina Rossetti

Love, affection, emotional bonding, the energy that seems to bring brighter colors, more intense satisfaction in everything we see, do, or touch . . . everyone searches for love. Can a talisman be made to aid us in this deep human need? Love talismans have been constructed since the dawn of time.

In creating a quilt to bring love to yourself, it is best not to have a specific person in mind. Instead, pray for a satisfying relationship that will meet your needs and those of your partner. A point of serious believers is not to involve others in intensive visualization without their permission. This can be thought of as a violation of free will—one of the foremost Wiccan principles is "Harm no one," as is "Be careful of what you ask for." Therefore, simply be open and receptive—picture someone who will be of like mind and pursuits. Often—and if we are lucky—we are brought what we need, rather than what we desire. It is up to us to discover the difference.

Can You Suggest a Ritual or Method That Will Help to Bring Loving Energies into My Environment?

Remember that love begins within yourself, and you must love yourself in order to be free to love another.

To bring or deepen love within your life, the following mixture may be simmered as you work on your talisman. Although the potpourri is very pleasant, the aroma should not be used for simple deodorization of the house! Each motion, item, and fragrance has its purpose—be mindful of this.

3	tablespoons rose petals, fresh or dried
2	tablespoons camomile (or one camomile tea bag, opened)
1	tablespoon coriander (whole is most fragrant)
1	tablespoon dried lavender
1	teaspoon ground cinnamon or 1 whole stick
½	whole vanilla bean or 2 tablespoons extract
½	teaspoon white sugar or honey

Stir these ingredients with the forefinger of your right hand, using a clockwise motion, in a china or silver bowl. Infuse the mixture with strong loving thoughts. Visualize an electric current full of the potential of your love flowing out of your finger and into the water.

Use an enamel or glass cooking pot. Metal may react with the herbs unfavorably. Set this container aside for this use exclusively. Add three cups of water, bring to a simmer. Pour in the herbal mixture slowly while repeating this formula:

Love awakens
In these rooms;
Come by the power
Of these blooms.

Or,

Love's sweet power
In my heart;
With this scenting
Let love start.

Do not boil the mixture, but keep at a temperature where a steady aromatic steam rises. Periodically add more water so that the pot does not boil dry. A commercial simmering potpourri container may be used, either electric-powered or candle-heated. Adjust the quantity of potpourri and water to suit the container. (Do not drink this mixture; protect it from pets and people.)

Set aside the hot mixture and let it cool when you put away your quilt. Add water and reuse the potpourri each day as you work on your talisman. Think of the steam and scent carrying the image of your worthiness and receptiveness to love into the atmosphere.

What Is a Magic Love Quilt Used For?

A love quilt will help you focus your energies to attract love and be more loveable. Concentrating your attention on increasing your own desirable qualities—such as compassion, empathy, tenderness, and sexuality—will enhance your attractiveness to one who is open to such positive characteristics.

How Long Will It Take to Make a Love Quilt?

The quilt should be constructed over the period of one lunar month to add the symbolic power of a lunar cycle to the composition. However, as with any human endeavor, time sometimes must be adjusted to the needs of the outer world. I consider the time that I cleanse my workbox as the beginning of my project.

When Is the Best Time to Start a Talisman to Increase Love?

Friday, the day of Venus, is the best general day to begin a magic love quilt. The planet of Venus rules love, peace, romance, acts of kindness, and home life.

There are other specific dates marking especially propitious days to begin a talisman for love. One such day would be March 5, the day of Isis, who is "she who binds hearts

Consider beginning your love talisman on September 1, the day of Radha, lover of the god Krishna.

together." March 9 is the celebration day of Aphrodite and her lover Adonis, and is unusual in that the goddess is part of a couple. This day is celebrated for success in union. March 17 is the festival of Astarte, a sacred day for the coming together of the male and female principles of the world.

February 14, popularly known as Saint Valentine's Day in the Christian feast-day calendar, was originally the Roman festival of Lupercalia. The wolf Lupa symbolized the breeding aspect of nature, fertility, and fecundity.

April 1 is the holiday of Venus or Aphrodite, the goddess of love and death. She can give happiness, love, and joy in relationships. April 30 is the Celtic festival of Beltain, celebrating the power and sacredness of sexuality. May 1 remembers the ceremonies of sacred dancing for the goddess Maia; the earth will be rewarded with abundant flowers and fruit as the result of nature's sexual union.

June 4 represents the Rosalia, the Roman Festival of Roses, worshipping Aphrodite, goddess of love. June 17 commemorates the marriage of Orpheus and Eurydice and is called "All Couples Day," the memorial of married love, loyalty, and faith to your chosen partner. June 21, Midsummer's Day, the sacred and powerful summer solstice, is a day for lovers worldwide; a time to preform divinations about love, and make midsummer wishes concerning love.

July 17 marks the marriage of Isis and Osiris. It is a day for celebrating marriages, sexual unions, and emotional commitments. September 1 is the day of Radha, lover of the god Krishna. This is a day to strengthen the shared love of couples.

Night, the time of the silver Moon, is the time to perform tasks that are associated with love, beauty, dreams, friendship, and peace. Summer is the season for love, marriage, and friendship. To begin this work when the Moon is in the sign of Cancer will add to the fruitfulness of your design. The Moon in Cancer will refresh that which has gone stale and enhance any quality of nurturing and emotional growth.

How Shall I Prepare My Workbox?

Select a new box made of sturdy paper or cardboard. The container may be of any shape, but should have a lid. I have seen many beautiful boxes in the local "dollar store" covered in reproduction Victorian papers patterned with cupids, roses, lace, and so on. Other boxes were covered in papers of red and pink roses, or mixed flowers. Any of these would be useful for your workbox, as would a plain white carton. Primarily, the container must be new and clean.

Cleanse your box using salt and sunshine as described in the chapter for health (Chapter Eleven). Empty and dispose of the salt, then add a generous pinch of white sugar to the box. Dust the sugar around into all the corners while picturing the goal you have in mind for constructing this quilt. Think of yourself as being worthy of love, as sweet and desirable as sugar.

Tip out the sugar onto a clean white piece of paper. Sprinkle the sugar grains under a growing plant in or near your home.

The workbox can be scented with one of the following fragrances. To increase attractiveness to males, use jasmine, neroli, tonka, lavender, or ambergris. To increase attractiveness to females, use violet, musk, or vertivert.

For a non-sex-specific scent that is a powerful love attractant, use the scent of red roses—rose oil may be used or red rose petals can be placed under folded white tissue paper on the bottom of the workbox. A small cloth bag filled with rose potpourri can be used if rose petals cannot be found.

Fresh rose blossoms should be thoroughly dried before using in this way. The flowers will stain your box and fabrics and turn moldy if any moisture is left in the petals. To dry a bloom, fill a shallow box with a mixture of 25% fine sand and 75% borax, which can be found in the laundry supply area of your grocery store. Put only the blossom (no stems or leaves) in the sand-borax mixture. Be sure the drying mixture is sifted between the petals, and into the flower. The container may be left uncovered in an airy, shady, dry area. Silica gel powder, which is used for a commercial drying agent, can also be used and may be found at craft and hobby shops. Silica gel is usually kept tightly covered, as the compound draws moisture from the air. Follow the enclosed instructions if you use such a product.

You may wish to dry other flowers for use in your talisman quilts. Not all types of flowers are suitable for drying with borax or silica gel. Other flowers that can be prepared by this type of desiccation are carnations, pansies, marigolds, larkspur, forget-me-nots, and zinnias. Treat the flowers very gently as the petals will be fragile after drying. Rose blossoms should take about a week to dry completely. The sand and borax mixture may be reused.

How Big Should This Love Quilt Be?

Because this quilt is so intimately associated with bodily reactions and sensations, I make love quilts big enough to lie on or cover up with. The size also reflects the spirit of generosity that you wish to cultivate in yourself and your lover.

What Shall I Visualize While I Work?

As you select your cloth and herbs, when you do your rituals, while you dress your candles, or write a note of your intentions, see with all the strength of your heart that overflowing of goodness in us all—the quality of love. When you project a radiant aura of love and generosity of spirit, a positive change will occur within you. Like stroking iron with a magnet, the force of your love will make you more loveable and attractive to another who is polarized in a receptive way.

Endeavor to literally impress your best qualities into your work. Visualize a pearly white luster of love for all illuminating your entire body. See the white light flowing from your fingers into the cloth. Think of something kind you have done. Picture a time you felt overwhelmed with love for something—a lover, a pet, a child, or a friend. Smile as you stitch. Have no stress, anxiety, or hate in your mind or heart as you stroke the cloth or press the herbs. Let the materials bring peace to you and love will follow.

What Materials Will Be Needed?

A love quilt will require you to select fabric, stones, herbs, and small items that carry the meaning of affection for you. This chapter will explain and list materials to help you make your choice. You will need candles, a workbox, sharp scissors, needles, sewing thread, pearl cotton thread, thimble, batting, and cloth for backing. When you empower your selected cloth, pure water, non-metallic pots, a new wooden spoon, salt, and herbs will be needed. If you decide to follow the suggestion of planting seeds, as presented later in this chapter, seeds and planting material (soil and pot) will be needed.

Please Suggest a Beginning Ritual for This Work.

This spell has been adapted from Scott Cunningham. Select three votive candles: red, pink, and white. You will also need a cinnamon stick, pink thread, a flame-proof trivet or tile, and a small piece of clean paper. Place the paper on the trivet and press your hand against the slip of paper firmly. Say these words:

> Love from above, love from below.
> Love from within, brings me love's glow.

Charge each candle with these words, the proper oil, and an inscription that represents your wish. Place the paper under the candle holder that holds the red candle and light the candles.

Hold the cinnamon stick carefully. Char the end of the spice in the flame of each candle in turn, starting with the red taper. Visualize as strongly as possible what you are requesting. The cinnamon stick will burn slowly. Let the spice flame for thirteen seconds (count to yourself). Blow the ember out gently. Lay the cinnamon on the tile or trivet and see that there is no live spark remaining.

As the cinnamon cools and the three candles are burning, assemble and hold the fabric you have selected for your quilt. Create a mental image of the type of person you wish to love and be loved by: someone kind, generous, strong, having the qualities you admire. Touch the fabric, stroke the cloth, and

Love from above, love from below. Love from within, brings me love's glow!

imagine yourself in affectionate and respectful interaction with this person. The repetition of thoughts will enable you to recognize the characteristics in a candidate for your love when he or she appears.

When the cinnamon has cooled, remove the paper from under the candle. Draw three hearts on the paper with the cinnamon sticks, one inside the other.

Then, wrap the pink string around the cinnamon stick. Give thanks for the help you are requesting and will receive. Leave the cinnamon on the paper in front of the candles until they burn out. When candles are spent, wrap the paper around the cinnamon stick and tie firmly with more pink thread. Place the wrapped spice stick in a small new envelope and put the amulet in your pocket or purse. Carry the envelope to remind you of your resolve to love and that you will be loveable.

On the last day of work on your quilt, include the wrapped spice stick in a hidden pocket of the charm.

If you prefer an alternate beginning ritual, the following will help dedicate your work to the Orisha Goddess Oshun. This ritual is to dispel evil and attract love.

Take a bath on each of five consecutive nights. Each night, place one of the following herbs in the bath water, in the following order: myrtle, vervain, lettuce, lavender, patchouli. After the initial herb is added, stir water well and add five tablespoons of honey, a large pinch of cinnamon, five egg yolks, and a small wine glass full of sweet red claret wine. Stir the water to a froth before entering the bath. Light two short yellow candles and call on the Orisha Oshun to grant your petition. Let these candles burn while you are bathing. To avert any possible allergic reaction, take a quick cool shower to rinse your body after the bath.

What Fabrics Shall I Use and What Designs and Images Should Be Included?

New fabric with the pattern of hearts, ivy, rings, pink or red roses or carnations, and fruit—especially apples—should be used. Do not use anything with white or yellow roses, although white or yellow daisies are permissible. Ivy represents the qualities of fidelity and faithfulness. Violets stand for kindness, steadfastness, and faith. Roses are a universal symbol of love and beauty.

An apple is a powerful fruit, strongly associated in history and folklore with deities such as Venus, Hera, Athena, and Diana, and is known as the Silver Bough or Fruit of Love. So strong is the magic of apples, the blood of the fruit—cider— may be used in place of blood or wine in rituals.

The prancing *chi-lin* (Chinese unicorn) gives longevity and happiness. Oriental images of rocks and clouds allude to the union of heaven and earth, male and female, and the delights of earthly sex. Delicate cherry blossoms are the images of new beginnings, springtime, brides, and unfolding happiness. Oak leaves and acorns stand for virtue, strength, and simplicity. Mandarin ducks depicted in pairs show marital fidelity and harmony between mates. Lush peony blossoms represent beauty, elegance, and the ideals of femininity. Pairs of cranes, often with necks intertwined, symbolize a long and harmonious relationship.

Delicate cherry blossoms can inspire new beginnings, springtime and unfolding happiness.

Patterns and images of any of the herbs and plants linked to love may be used, such as daisies, iris or pansy prints, or pictorial designs that display love-attracting herbs such as coriander, rosemary or catnip.

Cloth from favorite items of clothing of your own, especially those evoking happy memories, can be used. Fabric types that are associated with sensual pleasure such as silk, satin, and velvet may be added. Comforting emotions are produced with textures including flannel, plush, or artificial fur. All or any of these fabrics could be included, although these types of cloth are often difficult to sew due to their thickness.

What Plants and Herbs Shall I Use to Strengthen My Talisman?

Herbs and flowers to be included in a love quilt should be gathered or assembled for use on a Friday, if possible—especially a Friday that is within the period of time when the Moon is increasing. As the Moon increases, so will the effect of your wish. Luna will "draw" the effect desired as the Moon pulls the tide upward.

A spell cast in the increase of the Moon will cause growth; one cast in the decrease, or waning of the Moon, will cause a diminution or shrinkage. If you prefer to see your loneliness decreasing, enlist the power of the shrinking Moon.

Use the empowering technique and charge the fabric you have assembled for your use. Steep the cloth and dry the fabric in the moonlight. Herbs and flowers associated with the quality of love usually have a sweet or piquant scent.

Consider using some of the following herbs and flowers in your magic love quilt: bachelor's button flowers, daisy, lemon verbena, mimosa, marjoram, gardenia, caraway, coriander, cumin, jasmine, lavender, orris root, pink geranium, rose petals (especially red petals), rosemary, violets, yarrow, catnip, pansy. The dried plant matter, roots, leaves, or petals are used, as well as the image of the plant or blossom on the cloth.

Caraway (*Carum carvi*) is a masculine plant, and comes under the rule of the planet Mercury. The seeds are used to promote faithfulness in a partner. Chewing caraway seeds will help you to gain the affection of one you desire. Caraway enhances memory, cures fickleness, and promotes physical passion. Consider baking some caraway bread to present to the object of your devotion, as well as including the seeds within your quilt.

Cardamom (*Elettario cardamomum*) is a feminine plant under the auspices of Venus and the element of water. Fragrant cardamom is used in love potions, and can kindle lust if not used sparingly.

Catnip (*Nepeta cataria*) has the protection of the deity Bast, the great cat goddess of Egypt. Goddess Bast favors the plant with the power to enhance love, beauty, and happiness. The heart shaped leaves should be used in conjunction with rose petals. The inclusion of catnip in your work will delight your cat and add the extra kick of animal magic to the vitality of the charm.

Daisies (*Chrysanthemum leucanthemum*) bring physical love when worn. The bright-eyed flower is a flower of Venus. Add the figures of daisies to your quilt and

place pressed flowers between the layers of fabric.
Sleep with daisy root under your pillow (or in your
quilt) and a missing lover may return.

Iris (*Iris florentina*) is favored by the deities of love:
Venus, Isis, Osiris, Hera, and Aphrodite. Iris also
produces orris, the dried root of the iris plant, used
either whole or ground to a powder. To find and hold
love, the whole root can be added to a pocket in the
quilt, or the powder can be sprinkled on and between
the fabric. Orris root acts as a fixative for other scents,
as well. The image of this regal flower may be found
in cloth designs and incorporated into the quilt design.

Lavender (*Lavendula officinale*), rubbed on cloth, attracts
love and particularly fascinates men. Sprinkle a generous
portion of this delightful herb between the layers of
cloth. The scent of lavender has the power to conjure
memories of other times.

Lemon verbena (*Lippia citriodora* or *Aloysia truphylla*) is
a male plant that may be worn or carried to make the
owner desirable to the opposite sex. The lightly
lemon-scented plant is used in love potions, and if
added to other mixtures, increases their strength.
Rodale's *Encyclopedia of Herbs* calls the plant "an unas-
suming shrub, native to Chile and Argentina . . . . The
delicate lemony aroma is one that people seem to find
intimate." The plant will often have tiny lavender
flowers. Lemon verbena is an excellent addition to
mixtures to empower your cloth.

Lovage (*Levisticum officinale*) is known in English folklore
as the "loving herb." Lovage is used to bring true love
to the person who uses the plant. The stems and leaves
of the tall dark green herb look and taste like celery
and make a delicious addition to a salad, although the
fresh plant is sometimes difficult to find in United
States markets.

Add the dried lovage flowers, seeds, and leaves to
pockets in your quilt or place them between the
layers of fabric and batting.

For a cleansing and focusing ritual for one day of your work, use lovage and one other of the herbs mentioned in this list to prepare a bath by steeping a heaping tablespoon of fresh ground lovage root in two cups of boiling water. Add a large pinch of the second love-herb you select. Lavender is a good second choice for this bath. Allow the herb and ground root to steep for five minutes. Add the strained tea to a hot bath and mentally paint a detailed portrait of your future mate as the bath is washed over your body.

Roses are plants connected to the female aspect; the water element; and associated with the deities of Eros, Cupid, Demeter, Isis, and Adonis, among others. The flowers have a long history linking them with emotions, and in particular love. Include images of the striking blossoms and buds on the cloth and hide the dried petals between the layers of patches. To draw love, your fabric may be charged and empowered with rose petals, especially in addition to other herbs of your selection.

Vanilla's (*Vanilla aromatica*) scent and taste is thought to be lust inducing, so use with care. To sweeten your love, place a vanilla bean in your sugar bowl to infuse the powder with loving vibrations.

To use vanilla for a love talisman, tear a new, clean sheet of pink, white, or red paper into a heart shape. Write your name in the center of the heart. Sprinkle a pinch of the vanilla sugar over the paper. Fold the paper so no grains escape and wrap the packet with pink thread while picturing your lover's face. Place the little package in one of the secret wish pockets on your quilt. To remind you of your resolve, use the delicately flavored grains for cooking for yourself and your intended one.

Violets (*Viola odorata*), gentle purple flowers, protect against wicked spirits that may wish ill to the success of your talisman. Mixing the dried petals with lavender produces a love stimulant, so include them in small amounts.

Yarrow (*Achillea millefolium*, also called Devil's Nettle, Achillea, Arrowroot, Tansy) has a long history of association with witchcraft, healing, divination, and protection. Yarrow was a common herbal remedy for what was termed "female complaints," but gained a reputation as a plant that could be used for calling the spirits and as a flying herb. It is sacred to the goddess Venus and conveys the qualities of ardor, courage, and strengthening of psychic powers. The feathery leafed plant wards away evil thoughts and negativity.

To carry or wear yarrow brings love, attracts friends and draws the attention of those you desire to see, making this a quality you might wish to include in your talisman. Yarrow used in wedding decorations ensures at least seven years of love.

To remind you of your resolve, plant one or more of the herbs or flowers mentioned above. Most of the herbs, such as rosemary and catnip, grow easily from seeds in a regular garden pot. Before you plant the seeds, hold them in your hand and strongly visualize your request for love. Speak (out loud or mentally) to the seed and tell the little plant-to-be why you need its help. If you plant your herbs the day you begin your quilt, you will have a double reward of a flourishing plant and a finished talisman after thirty days.

As you tend the seeds and young plants, see the growth and progression of the sprout as the visible reminder that your invisible aura of love will also increase and thrive. Seeds need the powers of water (rain) and fire (sunshine), the same powers that control love. The sprouting of the plants is a manifestation of earth magic. If you neglect the little plant, so would you neglect your resolve to love and be loveable. The green shoot is a living reminder of your intent; a bloom is a promise of fulfillment.

I grow pots of geraniums, roses, tarragon, rosemary, oregano, mints, parsley, bee balm, and basil, as well as other common herbs, near my door. As well as being charming to the eye and raising the aura of protective house magic, the plants are readily available for craft magic and everyday cooking.

Rosemary has a particularly attractive aroma when burned. The incense-like silvery smoke dispels bad vibrations and negative thoughts. I throw a few snips into the fire when grilling to enhance the flavor of the meat and to adjust the attitude of the house and the cook. An old Scottish proverb says: "Where tha rosemary grows, tha mistress is master!"

Rosemary is very easy to grow. The piney fragrance can be used as a substitute for frankincense. A few twigs of the blue-green herb included in a flower arrangement enhances the pleasant smell and attracts additionally enjoyable thoughts of romance. The dried leaves dispel depression, lift the spirits, and make the soul open to the emotions that attract affection. Try cooking something delightful for your sweetheart with the fresh and fragrant sprigs. It is interesting that so many of the plants associated with love magic are common edible herbs!

Poppets, sometimes rather crudely called "voodoo dolls," can be made of cloth and stuffed with enchanted herbs and moss. The use of poppets is one of the oldest magical practices, and apparently has been done for over 4,000 years. The little figures are made to speed healing, or draw love or money. Sometimes a poppet is made of a root that has a human shape.

The common potato can be used as a poppet to represent yourself. Combined with the powers of rosemary, the following recipe gives you an interesting and tasty way to "bewitch" someone you would like to impress with your culinary powers. Perhaps having this dish for dinner before working on your talisman can serve as a beginning ritual. Do your work, be it cooking or sewing, with kindness and love foremost in your thoughts. The aroma of this dish is a love incense, and it is delicious.

Where tha rosemary grows, tha mistress is master!

—Scottish Proverb

Rosemary Potatoes

2	tablespoons butter
5, 7, or 9	small red potatoes (unpeeled)
	salt
	freshly ground pepper
1	tablespoon rosemary leaves (dried or fresh)

Melt 2 tablespoons of butter in the bottom of a baking dish. Preheat oven to 375 degrees. Scrub the small red potatoes, but do not peel. Slice potatoes carefully about ⅛ inch thick. Dip each slice into the melted butter, and arrange slices into concentric circles in the buttered pan. Sprinkle with salt, freshly ground pepper, and a generous amount (about 1 tablespoon) of dried or fresh rosemary leaves. Crush the rosemary between your palms and think of your partner as you sprinkle the herb over the vegetable. Bake until tops are golden brown, about 45 minutes.

Zsuzsanna Budapest (*Grandmother of Time*, HarperCollins, 1989) advises adding a tiny pinch of mugwort (*Artemisia absinthium*) to a dish you are cooking for an intended lover. Central European magic promises this herb makes the most frigid one of either sex amorous and virile.

Another food to remember in matters of love is lemon pie. This lover's dessert is a charm to strengthen faithfulness in a companion.

What Colors Will Aid My Goal of Attracting Affection?

The colors to attract love are—as you have probably suspected—pink, red, and white. Think of the hues of traditional Valentines.

Pink represents love, joy, happiness, romance, and pure feelings of affection.

Crimson red gives strength of will, warms the life force and aids ambition. This hot color should be included in a quilt to give energy, but must be balanced with the purple of intellect and wisdom. Thus, the power of sexuality imparted by the color red will be tempered into life-force energy rather than lust.

Red is the auspicious color of China, connoting happiness, warmth, strength, and fame. Red is the traditional color for brides and happy celebrations. Orange is thought of as a mixture of red and yellow, two deep power colors, and is imbued with the characteristics of both colors—power and happiness. Orange can intensify emotions, so it can be used in a love quilt, but in small doses. The "power" aspect of orange may also introduce a struggle between partners, so it should be used carefully.

Of particular interest is the shade of peach, denoting the quality of "peach blossom luck" to the Chinese. Peach is a good color for a single person, giving them attractiveness to the opposite sex. A single person with peach-blossom luck will have lots of friends and admirers. Most of the relationships will not last, but no one will be injured.

On the other hand, a married person with peach-blossom luck will be drawn toward adultery and will be destructive to marriage and the family. There can be violent quarrels, divorce, and even crimes of passion. In all, perhaps the shade of peach should be avoided in your quilt.

Include colors to induce wisdom and intelligence in order to be judicious in your choice in selecting a love. In every action it is necessary to be in tune and rhythm with yourself and nature. But let nothing be over-balanced, blinding you to the perfection of inner harmony.

Where Shall I Conceal My Secret Wishes?

Be sure to add several pockets to your quilt for charms, notes, and messages. Pockets can be of many different sizes and will act as containers to hold precious notes and mementos. I usually make several of these cloth envelopes in different sizes for the front and back of a quilt.

A rectangular piece of fabric may be folded like an envelope: dampen a paper envelope so that the glue loosens and carefully unfold the paper. Use the paper as your pattern to cut a piece of fabric to the proper shape. Fold the fabric in the same manner as the paper and press the cloth with your iron so that the folds remain crisp. You may wish to give the cloth a good spray of starch in order to hold the shape easily until you finish the envelope. Look at the unfolded paper and stitch on the cloth where the glue was on the paper (but do not sew the flap. Leave it open so you may conceal your secrets inside).

You may wish to add a button, snap, or ribbon tie so that the flap may be closed and opened at will, or simply sew the pocket shut once you have placed your inclusions within.

Other things that you wish to conceal completely and permanently may be placed between the quilt layers. Press the item to be hidden down gently into the batting cushion before covering and securing the little treasure with the fabric that will make a shield from curious eyes. Sometimes this will result in a small lump, which will add texture and interest and an air of magic and mystery to the surface of the quilt. Pockets sewn within garments may be used. Do not rip the pockets out, but instead cut the patch so that the pocket is included.

Are There Special Saints or Deities I May Petition for Help in This Quest?

The human drive for love, affection, and marriage has often been addressed to powerful goddesses and gods. This is only a partial list, but includes many of the most well-known divinities. Address a meditation to one of your choice as you work, include a dedication to this god or goddess within the embellishments or consecrate candles for the help of the powerful one as you work.

I often inscribe a short prayer or petition to a chosen goddess on the back of the quilt, using a fine tipped permanent-ink fabric marker, laundry marker or permanent ink quilt marker pen. When the wish is granted, I go back and add a thank-you note.

Aphrodite: (Greek, also known by the Roman name of Venus) goddess of love and beauty in all its aspects

Angus: (Celtic) god of love

Cupid: (Roman) also known as Eros, god of love

Cupra: (Etruscan) goddess of marriage and femininity

Cybele: (Roman, Phyrigian) goddess of passion and sexuality

Ishtar: (Babylonian) goddess of life and light; fecundity

Isis: (Egyptian) the mother-queen, she who binds hearts together, Nature

Juno: (Roman) goddess protector of women and marriage

Lakshmi: (East Indian) goddess of fertility and prosperity, shared love between couples

Maia: (Roman) goddess of spring, who brings forth life

Oshun: (West Indies) sea and water goddess of love and marriage; the joy in life, fertility

Okuninushi: (Japan) god and teacher; influential in matters of marriage and good fortune

Pan: (Greek) God that represents all that is male in the universe, a lover, male sexuality and virility

Saint Rita: saint who will address problems of loneliness and desperate situations

Saint Valentine: saint who is sympathetic to the unmarried

What Stones and Amulets are Useful for Attracting Affection?

Amethyst, a gentle violet stone, is a spiritual cleanser, gives tranquility, and eases stress and despair.

Dioptase is an emerald green silicate of copper. The mineral gem has the talent of healing those who feel emotionally abandoned. Dioptase heals the pains of heartache and allows one to reach out with trust.

Emerald, a very precious gem, opens the heart to peace and gentle emotions.

Blood dark garnet attracts love and promotes bonding, as well as increasing determination.

Lodestone, or magnet, "attracts" love. The Chinese name for lodestone is *t'su shi*, the loving stone.

Jade, particularly in certain animal shapes, is also a significant stone. A butterfly carved of jade is an emblem of successful love. A Japanese legend recounts the tale of a young man whose work and hobby was gardening. Luckily, his parents found a beautiful, quiet girl who shared a similar interest to be his wife. Together, they lived for each other and their exquisite garden. For

years they were childless, but then were blessed with
a son. He inherited his parents' passion for plants.
In old age, the parents died within days of each other.
The son cared for the garden, with love and respect
in his hands, thinking of the memory of his parent's
devotion. Each day he saw two graceful butterflies flut-
tering from flower to flower. As the seasons passed, the
son tended the blossoms the butterflies favored.
In the lengthening days of summer, he lay down to
rest on the wooden veranda. He slipped into sleep
and dreamed that his parents had returned and
were walking around the garden, admiring his diligence.
Suddenly, the pair turned into butterflies, and continued
the tour of the swaying blooms. In this way, the faithful
son knew the souls of his parents rested in the butterflies, and still enjoyed the solace of the garden.

A rooster carved of jade recalls a Chinese legend of a
beautiful white cock. When the cock saw its young
mistress fling herself into a well in despair over the loss
of her lover, the faithful pet followed her in death. Thus,
the figure of the jade rooster symbolizes faithful love.

Silver-white moonstone heightens sensitivity, soothes
a tendency to overreaction, and gives an offering of
peaceful serenity. Moonstone arouses the tender passions and gives lovers the ability to read the future of
the affair, if it be good or ill. To use this ability, the
stone must be placed in one's mouth when the Moon is
full. The opalescent moonstone acts as a mediator
between mind and emotions, encouraging beneficial
personal attachments. The gem will animate a search
for humanitarian devotion, romance, and sensitivity in
a partner. On the other hand, hard black onyx will cool
passion and provoke discord.

Opal, mysterious and ever changeable, is useful only to
those who have a birthday in October, but if this is
your birthday it can be a stone of romance.

Rose quartz stimulates a feeling of oneness with nature,
and opens the spirit for a loving, positive outlook.

Rose quartz gives emotional balance and establishes love and friendship. The translucent pink stone is sometimes called the Venus or love stone.

Shells from the sea may be used as amulets and placed in or on the quilt. Clam shells represent femininity and love. Conch are used for love magic and rituals in the Caribbean. Oysters represent love and good fortune as well as carrying reputed aphrodisiac qualities.

Blue-green turquoise, stone of the American desert, vibrates to the heart chakra, and aids love, soothing of pain, and gives stability to the emotions.

What Traditional Quilt Patterns and Superstitions are Thought to be Related to Love or Marriage?

The art of quilting has many time-honored superstitions regarding both the quilt pattern and the quilt itself. Perhaps because quilts were—and still are—common bed-furnishings the most prevalent superstitions concern the power to predict the future in relation to marriage, love, and motherhood.

- Shake a new quilt out the front door. The next person to come in will be the one you will marry.

- As soon as a quilt is taken off the frame, the cover must be wrapped around an unmarried woman to give her the luck to find a mate. The new quilt can also be thrown around the first unmarried man to "come in from the fields," to charm him into a relationship, as well.

- If you break a needle while quilting, the next new baby will be yours. A prick with the needle while quilting means a kiss given under the covers.

- Put the last stitch in a quilt sewn with other workers and you'll be the next to acquire a mate.

- A cat tossed on the new bedcloth will leap toward the person who will be married first in the future.

- A warning not to work on the Christian Sunday was reinforced by the admonition that any stitches put in

on a Sunday would have to removed with the seamstress' nose before she could take her place in Heaven.

- If the coverlet was to be used as a utility quilt, not put
  away for a impending marriage, the honor of being
  first to sleep under the handiwork was coveted as that
  night's dream would give a glimpse of the future. If the
  dreamer was unmarried, the life's-partner could be
  seen that night.

- An unmarried girl should produce a dozen quilt tops
  before her marriage, but they should not be quilted
  until after the engagement was formalized. A thir-
  teenth top—the magic number—could then be made
  and quilted by her friends.

Often a deliberate mistake was introduced into a meticu-
lous pattern to show that the maker had a humble spirit, and
none but the Deity could produce a perfect work. This bit of
lore seems to reflect the tale of the proud weaver who challenged the Goddess to a weaving contest. The unfortunately
boastful mortal was changed into a spider to spend her days
spinning and weaving for the rest of her life.

There are many folk beliefs about quilt patterns in association with love and marriage. "Turkey Tracks" promoted a
wandering spirit and unfaithful husband. "Drunkard's Path,"
although beautiful and requiring a deft seamstress, was
thought to possibly bring the curse of drunkenness to the
home. More acceptable patterns for a dowry were "Bridal
Stairway," "Honeymoon Cottage," or "Cupid's Arrowpoints."

For a skilled quiltmaker, the "Double Wedding Ring" pattern is perfect. The graceful circles of interlocked rings symbolize eternity and love, making it a customary wedding gift.
Experts disagree on the origin of the pattern, but the romantic
connection of the quilt has carried over for at least two centuries. Some point to the sixteenth-century gimmal betrothal
rings as the prototype for this quilt design.

The beauty of the elaborate appliqué of a Pennsylvania
Bride's quilt is stunning. The pattern combines the design
elements of traditional love talismans of doves, hearts, ribbons, and complicated arrangements of lush flowers. This

pattern, however, takes an excessive amount of time and a great amount of skill and patience.

A simple image of the happy home can be produced with the easy log-on-log strip construction of "The Log Cabin." The central "hearth-fire" of the square is usually red or orange to represent the live fire within the protective walls.

What Ideograms Shall I Use to Represent My Wish?

Chinese characters that may be included in this talisman include *ai*, love; *fu*, happiness; *jen*, patience; *shun*, gentleness; *mei*, beauty; *shih*, honesty; and *ho*, harmony.

Love, *ai*, infers the feeling of love as a highly spiritual emotion, a form of giving. Above and below the brush strokes for "heart" the characters for "graceful movement" and "breath" are painted to see love as an inspiration, drawing the breath of life to the heart and grace to the body.

A saying of the sage Confucius related that happiness, *fu*, comes not from material things but from the harmonious inner life.

Patience, *jen*, is written with the pictograph of a knife blade bearing upon the heart. Yet the heart endures. Jen can be read as "tolerance," as a firm heart is a tolerant one. Both patience and tolerance are needed to love freely and wisely.

Ho is the Chinese ideogram for harmony.

What Stitching Patterns Shall I Use to Finish the Piece?

Stitching patterns may include the symbols of love: rings, twining vines and flowers, the heart, clasped hands, two hearts linked together, doves, ribbons tied into bows, and interlocking circles. The stitches are representative of knot magic. As you sew you are binding your intentions into the fabric of the quilt. Stitch with patience and love.

Knots are tokens of unity and harmony between mates. A ring is an ancient symbol of eternity. Acorns show promise of new and strong life from union.

Hearts indicate devotion, love, and faithfulness. An elderly friend advised that hearts should only be stitched on a quilt intended "for love." As for her, she used a pattern of spider webs for her quilts!

Of course, include an outline of your hand in the stitching if you have not added the silhouette elsewhere on the quilt.

After all quilting has been completed, lay the quilt out flat on the floor or other wide flat surface. Look at the cloth and check that everything is in place to your liking. If extra stitching, color, or embellishments are needed, now is the time to decide on these. Meditate on your purpose and resolve on constructing this talisman. If all is as you wish, trim the edges straight and bind them or use the pillowcase finish method. Add hangers or loops (as described on pages 34 and 35) if you intend to hang or display the quilt.

What Fragrance Will Add an Aura of Love Attraction to My Construction?

By now you will notice, if you hold your quilt against your face, that the cloth has gained a faint distinctive scent that is a combination of the physical components of your creation such as the herbs and flowers used to charge the fabrics, the hidden plant matter, even the paper, stones, and candle wax. Your workbox will add a certain faint note, as will your own hands and the thoughts that you have so diligently placed within your composition. The final touch that you may wish to add to your quilt is a scent that is symbolic of the intent within the fabric and stitches.

Aromas and herbs associated with love are usually fruity, flowery, and sweet. The scent of roses is used in all and any love intention. Apple blossoms are traditional to promote love, happiness, and success. Orange blossom, known in old magic as "man trap," builds personal attractiveness. A drift of orange blossom on the breeze creates the mood for matrimony.

Jasmine, symbol of the Moon, attracts spiritual love, and is also said to be a magnetic oil to attract men. Neroli, tonka, lavender, and ambergris are other herbal pheromones to attract the male of the species. The oils of musk, vertivert, and violet attract women. The sharp tang of red carnations, in scent or dried as an herbal addition to the love quilt, will add sexual energy, as does ginger.

Pick only the oils with perfumes that blend pleasantly and not too strongly.

What Shall I Do with My Talisman Now That I Am Finished? What Is My Closing Ritual to Set the Energies in Motion?

Once more, lay your beautiful talisman out before you. Meditate on your purpose in making it. Think of the time you have spent and prayers you have made. Touch the cloth, press the mysterious bumps, and hear the tiny crinkly noises where your powerful wishes and desires are hidden in the folds and pockets.

Decide how you will use your talisman to the best advantage. A love talisman could be hung so that you can see the bright banner as you do your daily work, as a reminder to endeavor to be open and loving in your life. You may prefer to fold your magical work carefully in the scented box, nestled in fresh tissue, to be taken out and held as you visualize the materialization of your desires. You may wish to drape a love quilt over the foot of your bed, to draw over your body as you dream.

When you have made the decision of where your talisman should be kept, it is time to perform a final ritual that will both put a sense of closure to the project, and set wings to your intentions. Picture the power of your unlocked energies flying away to achieve what you need.

At night, spread the quilt on your bed. Light three candles in this room: pink, red, and white. Charge each candle by sending your wishes into the energy flow of your environment. Picture those wishes and desires as strongly and as clearly as you can. Place a fragrant bouquet of fresh flowers nearby and add fresh rosemary sprigs if they are available. Let the candles be the only source of light in the room. Place the tapers or votives in a safe place, as they should be allowed to burn completely without interruption. Avoid anything that might tip or blow over, or anything excessively dry. Use a hurricane glass shield over the candles if necessary.

The scent of neroli and lavender are magnetic oils of male attraction.

While the candles are burning, take the remains of your potpourri outside and pour it under the largest tree available. Request the spirit of the tree to accept your offering.

Scour the potpourri pot thoroughly.

Take a warm bath, by candlelight if possible, using three drops of the oil you have chosen to scent your quilt in the bath water. While bathing, endeavor to picture yourself as receiving what you have wished for. Visualize the goddess or god to whom you have directed your desires reading the wishes you have written.

Tonight if there is moonlight, allow it to shine into your room. Check that the candles are burning safely. Slip into bed under your magic quilt. If you are feeling adventurous, sleep in the nude tonight. Tell yourself that you will dream of love and make it so.

When you awake in the morning, the spell has been set free to do its work.

From time to time, after you have finished any talisman, it is good to recharge the magic by exposing the work to the light of the Moon on a solstice. This is especially necessary if you feel the charm has been working heavily or has been exposed to bad influences.

Summary

Day to Begin

Friday: Day of Venus—preferably on a summer night when the Moon is in the sign of Cancer

Significant Dates

February 14: Lupercalia, Saint Valentine

March 5: Day of Isis

March 9: Aphrodite and Adonis

March 17: Festival of Astarte

April 1: Venus, Aphrodite

April 30: Beltain

May 1: Maia (May Day)

June 4: Rosalia, Aphrodite

June 17: Marriage of Orpheus and Euridice, All Couples Day

June 21: Midsummer's Day, Summer solstice

July 17: Marriage of Isis and Osiris

September 1: Radha and Krishna

COLORS

orange: energy, power, happiness

pink: joy, love, romance, pure feelings of affection

purple: intellect, wisdom, the spirit

red: strength of will, energy, sexual love, passion

white: peace, the spirit

FABRIC MOTIFS

acorns: promise of new life

apples: the fruit of love, Venus

carnations: energy

fruit: plenty, fruitfulness

hearts: love, devotion, faithfulness

ivy: fidelity

knots: unity, harmony between mates

rings: eternity

red roses: love, beauty

violets: kindness

IDEOGRAMS

beauty

gentleness

happiness

harmony

honesty

love

patience

STONES AND NATURAL AMULETS

violet amethyst: eases stress and despair, spiritual cleanser

dioptase: heals the pain of heartache, gives trust

emerald: peace, gentle emotions

garnet: attracts love, promotes bonding

jade: successful love

lodestone: attracts love

moonstone: peaceful serenity, arouses tender passion, encourages beneficial personal attachments

opal: romance

rose quartz: opens spirit for a loving outlook

turquoise: aids love, heals and helps the heart, gives emotional stability

HERBS AND FLOWERS

bachelor's button, daisy, lemon verbena, mimosa, marjoram, orris root, pink geranium petals, red rose petals: love

caraway: faithfulness, gaining affection

cardamom: love potions, lust, sensuality

catnip: animal power, enhancer of beauty and happiness

lovage: brings true love

rosemary: love potions, dispels negativity

yarrow: strengthens ardor and courage

FRAGRANCES

apple blossoms: season of spring, marriage

red carnation: energy

jasmine, neroli, tonka, lavender, ambergris: increases attractive vibrations to males

orange blossom: marriage, builds personal attractiveness

rose: giving and receiving love, romance

rosemary: attracts thoughts of romance, dispels bad thoughts

violet, musk, vertivert: increases attractive vibrations to females

STITCHING PATTERNS

acorns: promise of new life

hearts: love, faithfulness, devotion

interlocking rings, circles, clasped hands: love, faithfulness, eternity

knots: harmony between mates

rings: eternity

Chapter 7

A Gift of Love for Love

Giving from the Heart

Love one another, but make not a bond of love: Let
it rather be a moving sea between the shores of
your souls.

—Kalil Gibran

*I*n order that the process of constructing a talisman quilt
will be more clear, in this chapter I describe the process
I used to design a love talisman quilt for a friend as a wedding gift. From selecting the day to begin through finishing
the quilt for hanging, each step is detailed. The quilt would
be a magic amulet to draw additional loving energies and
feelings of harmony to the union.

Selecting a Day to Begin

The wedding would be in late April, but in order to allow
myself ample time to finish, I planned to begin in early March.
A study of the calendar and almanac showed March 5 (the day
sacred to Isis, she who binds hearts together) to fall on the day
of a full Moon. This was a good day to begin, although it was
not a Friday (day ruled by the planet Venus). Had there not
been a good festival, such as the Festival of Isis, I would have
simply selected a Friday on the increase of the Moon.

Preparing the Workbox

For a workbox, I purchased a new blanket-sized box at a gift wrap store. The shiny silver paper covering the box was impressed with wedding symbols—doves, bells, bows, and flowers—and would serve as a presentation container when I was finished with the quilt. I cleansed the box with salt and sunshine, and then added an additional cleansing and blessing for love by adding sugar in the same manner.

Earlier in the year I had saved roses from a wedding shower for the bride-to-be and dried them in silica gel powder so that the blossoms were ready to be used in the workbox and in the quilt. I sprinkled red rose petals and rose potpourri on the bottom of the box and covered them with several folds of white tissue paper.

Selecting the Cloth

I bought strips and squares of pink, red, and white cloth (love, happiness, and purity), as well as one and a half yards each of white cotton muslin and a fleece-thickness batting for the body of the quilt. The white muslin would provide the backing, leaving a clear place for me to write good wishes and a spell for happiness after I'd finished all the sewing. I selected several yards of narrow ribbon in orange (energy and happiness), crimson (life warmth and ambition), and purple (wisdom and spirituality).

Finally, I bought new fabric with red and pink roses (love, happiness) twined with ivy (faithfulness). A yard of plain black cotton fabric would make up the border, framing the inner composition and serving as a protective force. It would also be a representative of the water (feminine) force of nature. I would also use this black fabric for the calligraphic ideograms.

I added snips and strips of cloth from the bride's wedding dress, and sections and pockets from her favorite pair of jeans and from the groom's old baseball shirt.

My Beginning Construction Ceremony

I began my composition by completing the ritual of candles and smoldering cinnamon (as presented on page 69), adding the names of the bride and groom rather than my own. I visualized the two in a happy and fruitful marriage and especially as good friends who would learn to treasure each other even more as the years passed.

Empowering the Cloth

I dedicated the cloth to Isis, who would protect and nurture. Because the day I chose to begin was the day of the full Moon (beginning the decrease of the Moon), the union was depicted as dissolving opposition and differences to form a new entity.

To charge and empower the cloth, I selected lemon verbena (male, increasing attraction to the opposite sex, augmenting power of other herbs), rosemary (female, opens the soul to affectionate emotions, lifts depression) and catnip (goddess Bast, enhancement of love and beauty, animal energy). After the cloth dried in the moonlight, the charged fabric was pressed and folded in the workbox. Yarrow (goddess Venus, courage, warding of evil thoughts), dried violets (charm against jealous spirits that may wish ill to the success of the charm), and lavender (male attractant) were collected for later use within the layers of the quilt.

The same day that I empowered the cloth, I planted pots of rosemary, yarrow, and catnip as gifts for the couple in their new home.

Preparing the Base of Backing and Batting

The next step was to prepare the backing and batting so that I would have a base on which to construct the quilt. I pinned a layer of the fleece polyester batting to the muslin, placing safety pins 6 to 8 inches apart. The quilt would be a rectangle, 45 inches wide and 60 inches long. I folded the rectangle into quarters and marked the center point with a colored pin as a reference point for the placement of the central patch.

Start in the Center

I began by placing a handpainted fabric valentine on the center mark of the batting. Because this central motif would be the focal heart of the quilt, I gave a lot of thought as to what to place under the lavender and pink painted square. First I wrote a simple petition to Isis, the Mother-queen of nature and love, for this union to be blessed by the grace of shared love. I folded this paper around a heart-shaped bit of polished moonstone, the opalescent gem that soothes tendencies to overreact, arouses the tender passions, and animates romance. The thread and paper wrapped cinnamon stick was also placed under this central square.

I then pinned the fabric square with straight pins around all four sides to keep the hidden paper and stones in place until the next section of fabric was added.

Surrounding the Central Panel

Next, I pinned a strip of satin from the bride's wedding dress with the right side against the painted square, and sewed down the pinned edge. I removed the pins at the sewn edge and smoothed over the satin strip by hand (do not iron) and pinned at the unsewn edge. Satin strips were sewn in the same manner around the remaining three sides of the central painted square. The shiny satin not only gave a pleasing visual contrast to the dull finish fabrics, but is also a cloth associated with pleasure. These white strips were made wide enough to serve as a background for the ideograms.

Continuing to Build Outward

Next, I added strips from the groom's baseball shirt and placed a selection of herbs under each strip after the strip had one side sewn. I patted the herbs in place on the batting and laid the fabric over the leaves and pinned the raw edge. I used dried daisy petals to strengthen physical love and violet leaves to protect against ill wishes under this round of fabric.

The third section of cloth was added by cutting long strips from an old pair of jeans belonging to the bride, leaving the pockets intact. These strips were pinned in sequence to the pinned sides of shirt pieces and sewn down. Then lovage leaves (love), red rose petals (love), sugar (gentleness and love), and salt (protection) were sprinkled on the batting that would be underneath. The denim was then folded over the herbs, patted into place, and pinned.

The next rounds of fabric included empowered new cloth of solid red (passion), solid pink (love and happiness), designs of red and pink roses (love) and twining ivy (virility and faithfulness), and a print of apples and grain (prosperity and love). Yarrow leaves and flowers were sprinkled under this fabric. When a width of fabric had been built that was aesthetically pleasing to me (about ⅔ of the total piece), I decided to add the border.

I measured the area of batting remaining to be covered and cut strips of new black cloth charged for protection. When the sections of black cloth were sewn on, the batting and backing were completely covered.

Please note that all this was not done on one day, but accomplished in steps over the period of a lunar month. Do not rush through your projects, but work with thought, pleasure, and consideration in each step. The love in the construction will benefit your well-being as well as the recipient.

The Quilting Pattern

In one corner, I outlined my right hand, tracing around each finger and the palm with a sliver of soap. Then, tracing around a teacup as a guide, I made a pattern of interlocked rings around the entire outside border. This is the American traditional "Double Wedding Ring" pattern or the Oriental "linked gems" motif. Using the soap sliver, I drew a heart, a knot, and two acorns in the remaining corners.

Since the fabric was dark, I used white pearl cotton thread so that the stitches would show. Following the soap outlines, I stitched through all three layers—top fabric, batting, and backing muslin—in an even running stitch.

Before attaching the embellishments, I selected three Chinese ideograms to be placed in three corners of the white satin. I made two copies of the calligraphic characters for love, happiness, and harmony. Each character was enlarged slightly in order to make the small pieces easier to work with.

Using Wonderunder, a fabric bonding film, I fused the black cotton cloth and the pattern for the ideograms together. I cut the pieces apart, one ideogram at a time, and used one copy for a pattern in order to place the strokes correctly. To avoid disappointing mistakes, I tested the fusing material, heat of the iron, and the black fabric on a scrap of the material to bond to (in this case, the white satin). The placement of the calligraphy makes a dramatic focal statement, so you may wish to test several placements before you iron the characters on permanently.

Embellishments

A trip to the craft store yielded a selection of small polished gemstones—rose quartz (opens spirit for a loving outlook), turquoise (emotional stability, good health) and garnet (determination, love, bonding) were all sewn into the design.

At an Oriental import store I purchased a green jade butterfly and a small jade rooster (successful married love and devotion) and a pewter charm of Kwan Yin, Goddess of Mercy. Ribbons of purple (intellect and wisdom) and orange (energy and passion) were braided, used to fasten the charms, and left with long tails to add texture and movement to the surface of the quilt. In addition, three small mirrors to deflect sadness and ill wishes were sewn on the front of the quilt.

I made cloth envelopes using new fabric printed with big red apples and apple blossoms (fruit of the deities of love, Venus, Hera, and Athena), as well as fabric envelopes of bridal satin. One envelope held a copy of the wedding invitation, another contained a photograph of the bride and groom and a special prayer written for the occasion. The envelopes were sewn on the front of the quilt. The pockets of the blue jeans were left open and empty so that the bride and groom could place their personal wishes in these hiding spots.

Finishing the Edges

One edge of my construction was somewhat uneven so I laid a yardstick over the edge and marked a straight line, then trimmed away uneven edges following the line. Using red wide-width bias binding, I bound all four edges following the instructions on the binding packet.

Finishing the Back

Using a fine-tipped permanent marking pen, I wrote a brief wish for the happiness of my friends. I added my name as the maker, the date of construction, and the date of the wedding.

Final Finish

The bride had expressed her wish to use the quilt as a wall hanging in her new home. After checking for any dangling threads or forgotten pins, I added silver clip-on curtain hooks at the top of the quilt.

I tucked a small ball of cotton touched with a drop of red rose oil (for love) into the bottom of one of the jeans pockets. The quilt was wrapped in new white tissue paper and placed in the silver box, which would now be the gift box. I tied pink and silver ribbon around the container, added sprigs of orange blossoms and rose buds, and presented the talisman at the ceremony.

Chapter 8

A Quilt for Inner Harmony

A Talisman for Serenity and Balance

Be still
and discover your center of peace.
Throughout Nature
The Ten-thousand things move along,
But each returns to its source.
Returning to the center is peace.

—Tao 16

Harmony, the quality of serenity and balance, is a pool of inner calm that is necessary for a full and rewarding life. Tranquility in the midst of turbulent times is necessary, but often difficult. Sometimes harmony is brought about by an acceptance of what cannot be changed. Often serenity can be achieved by examination of our spiritual life and adjusting its physical expression. Gaining harmony in your personal life is a goal that most of us set, but don't always achieve. After a particularly trying day, I wrap my harmony quilt around my shoulders, drape the cloth over my lap, or kneel on the quilt as I concentrate on my meditation.

Create a time to think about what you want to accomplish. Visualizing yourself practicing that virtue with ease is an important step toward gaining the talent you desire. As an athlete will concentrate on the perfect performance, and when challenged can respond correctly, you can create much the same effect. Tranquil balance is not the unresponsive state of an oyster, but the relaxed, alert posture of a samurai warrior, capable of great feats, in harmony with his world.

While working on a harmony wish quilt, think of building the balance in your life as you build the composition, piece by piece. Picture peace surrounding you. Envision yourself as a source of serenity, affecting all that is near you.

How Shall I Endeavor to Bring Harmony into My Environment?

If your home environment seems a particular source of discord, investigate the principles of *feng shui* in order to bring the forces of nature into balance within your living space. As a beginning into this ancient practice of harmony, consider the color of your front door. A white door can be a "doorway to sadness," as white is considered a color of mourning and death in China. In practical application, a dirty door covered with grime, chipped, and worn, does not give the picture you wish to receive from the welcoming portals of your sanctuary.

Tend what is around you and your life will absorb the vigor and energy of the universe in harmony.

Scrub the entrance of your home until every crack is clean and allow the door to dry. Paint the door in a color recommended for balance and happiness. Green, blue, and red are colors considered auspicious for entrances; Chinese temple doors are painted vermillion to ward off dark evil. Cast handfuls of salt around and across the steps and project your resolve not to allow discord to enter. Sprinkle again with sugar to draw happiness and wealth. There should be no clutter or disorder near the entrance or hallway.

Look at your lawn and plants. Is the foliage brown, dry, and dying, indicating the diminution of life force and nature? When a plant thrives, so will the owner. Healthy leaves are the color of healthy life force, *ch'i*. Tend what is around you and your life will absorb the vigor and energy of the universe in harmony.

During the week that you begin your creation of this talisman, make a point to select some items around your home that you no longer use. Discard, to a recycler such as Goodwill, at least one item a day in a literal, conscious effort to simplify your life and gain order within.

When Is the Most Auspicious Time to Begin?

Work for inner harmony is best begun on Monday, the day of the Moon, in order to enhance the feelings of spiritual attainment and self-confidence. Either the full or new Moon is optimum, depending on whether you see your quality of harmony as building with the growing Moon or as an element of disharmony diminishing with the reducing lunar disk.

January 30 and June 3 correspond to the Roman festivals of Pax, the goddess of peace. February 22 is the feast of good friends, the feast of Concordia, the Roman personification of harmony—it is a time to make peace.

May 19 is the time of cleaning of sacred places, the festival of Kallyntaria (Greek). Sacred things were washed and refurbished in solemn rededication.

A personal favorite date is May 25, celebration of the Tao, Mother of the World. In Taoism the One Goddess is seen as the mother of the world. The Chinese mystic philosophy of the Tao is a respect for truth and harmony in nature; the Goddess is the way to the heart.

How Shall I Prepare My Workbox?

A workbox for a harmony talisman should be white, gray, blue, or a shade of purple such as lilac. The container may also be rainbow-striped, as the rainbow is the symbol of Nature's power to bring life into harmony and a charm to change your luck. The box may be of new paper or wood such as cedar or sandalwood.

Cleanse the workbox with salt and sunshine and add a fragrance of gardenia, lilac, rose, cumin, or cloves.

How Big Shall I Make This Quilt?

For a harmony quilt, size is an option to be decided by the maker. I like to have my personal quilt large enough to drape over my lap or to sit upon during meditation, approximately 45 inches square. If you decide to use your harmony talisman as a meditation mat, remember to put any embellishments toward the edges of the quilt so that your thoughts will not be disrupted by sitting on lumps. You may wish to make your quilt small enough to use as a scarf over your altar area or as a wall hanging.

What Shall I Concentrate on While I Work?

Think about what is disturbing about your environment or relationships. Picture a balance scale and see yourself placing the elements of your life upon the golden pans: work, money, love, children, your relationship with others and nature itself.

What is on each side that would tip over the scales from one side to another? Is something needed? Or should something be deleted? Too many thoughts of work and not enough time with yourself? In order to build serenity and harmony within your life, sometimes it is necessary to subtract some elements. Too much noise that makes confusion in your thoughts and not enough calming sounds?

Think about the definition of harmony—several tones blended into a pleasing whole. Meditate on bringing the disparate parts of your life into a melodious chord. Should the emphasis on one part of your life and environment be "lowered" or "turned up"? As you select the components of your harmony talisman, picture the parts of your life coming together to make a coherent whole.

What Materials Are Needed for This Project?

As you select your cloth, herbs, and colors, remember the importance of keeping your symbols consistent in meaning. Energy, like a light beam, is more powerful when the stream is tightly focused and aimed into the target of your desire.

Gather scissors, needles, sewing thread, and cloth for your project. Batting, pins, and backing cloth will also be needed. Read this section carefully and make a list of your selections of candles, colors, herbs, stones, and so on that you will want to use. In a construction for achieving harmony, planning before beginning is particularly important so that the effort moves forward smoothly, without frustration or impediments. Let all motion be part of your resolve and visualization to enlarge the harmony in your life.

Please Suggest an Opening Ritual to Dedicate My Work.

As a beginning for this project, I recommend a ritual given by Scott Cunningham, a "Peace Bath." The ceremony will help you center yourself and relax.

Read the process below in full and gather the materials needed. Place them on a blue, violet or white cloth. A bath towel will do, as the ritual will be done in the bathroom.

Take off all your clothes. Draw a warm bath for yourself. Play a tape of soothing nature noises such as water, birds, or rain.

Three candles are needed: one blue, one white, and one pink. A blue candle is lit to increase the spirit of patience and happiness. A white candle is used for purification. Light a pink candle to increase the aura of relaxation.

Prepare to light these candles by holding them one by one between your palms. Visualize your goal of inner harmony in any way that seems most symbolic to you. The image may be a scene of yourself sitting on a park bench in peaceful relaxation or a more active picture of yourself performing a task in confidence.

Make the picture complete in your mind in every detail. Light the candles one by one. Do not rush.

Take a china, wooden, or silver bowl half-full of water and pour in a tablespoon of milk. As you do so, say out loud:

Water ripples on the breeze . . .

Add several (or a handful if they are available) rose petals, fresh or dried, to the bowl. Swirl the bowl and say:

Thistledown flies through the air . . .

Stir the water, milk and rose petals with the index finger of your right hand, clockwise, and say:

Silent as the mighty seas . . .

Gently pour the mixture into your bath and repeat:

Peaceful here without a care.

Step into the bath, soak and relax. Picture the water melting away any trouble or tension in your life. After you have completed your bath, if the candles have not burned out, carry them into your work area to illuminate your thoughts as you compose your quilt. Do not reuse them for another purpose; it is best to let them burn out completely.

What Fabrics Shall I Use?

New fabrics and materials should be used for this quilt to symbolize your resolution to cast out old bad thoughts and habits that cause disharmony in your life.

What Fabric Designs and Motifs Shall I Incorporate?

Use fabric with roses, which bring feelings of calm and release of personal stress. Passion flowers give peace and calm troubles.

Five bats indicate the Five Chinese Blessings: Happiness, Peace, Virtue, Wealth, and Longevity. The Chinese word for bat is *fu*, a word that sounds like the written character for happiness. Including cloth with patterns of bats (plentiful around Halloween) will bring happiness, a necessary quality for harmonious living.

Fish are the Chinese charm to avert all evil, bringing wealth, married joy, and harmony. The mighty carp, famed for swimming upstream against any obstacle, is a symbol of perseverance and the ability to overcome the struggles of life.

A design of mountains and water symbolizes the balance of the masculine yang force (mountain) and feminine yin (water.) Use this motif if your serenity is unbalanced due to an interpersonal conflict.

Water is the element of peace, and the symbols, patterns, and colors of water are appropriate for seeking tranquility. Fabric with designs of waves should be used. An experienced quilter could attempt a pattern with gentle undulations.

Include in this, and any other of these quilts, a tracing of your hand either appliquéd, glued, painted, or stitched. Shapes, initials, and designs personally significant to the maker, perhaps the graceful dove of peace, should be incorporated.

What Herbs and Flowers May Be Used for Empowering My Talisman for Harmony?

Include pinches of leaves or pressed dried flowers in secret seams and pockets of your composition, or rinse the cloth in an empowering infusion of the herbs and blossoms. If an herb or flower that particularly draws you is unavailable in fresh or dried form, use an image of the plant.

Aloe is a plant that has been used for centuries. One species of aloe (*Aloe barbadensis* sp. aloe vera) is well known as a healing herb. The thick-leafed plant is filled with juice useful for physical and spiritual medicine, giving patience and protection. Because of the fleshy texture of aloe, the leaves are unsuitable for inclusion within the harmony quilt. Instead, anoint and purify your hands with aloe juice before starting your work.

In India and China, the fragrant aloe (*Aloe arborescens*) is used to purify the soul. Other varieties of the aloe are used for amulets and talismans to avert evil and are used for the invocation of helpful spirits. In Mexico the aloe agave (*Sabila sagrada*) is home to a powerful goddess who can bestow health, wealth and peace.

Bay (*Laurus nobilis*) and **cloves** (*Syzygium aromaticum*) ward off negativity, either directed toward you or originating from your own thoughts. Bay, cloves, basil (*Ocimum basilicum*), and cumin (*Cumimum cyminum*) will most likely be found on your spice shelf. Include a healthy scattering of these herbs between the layers of fabric for peace of mind, love and happiness.

Camomile (*Anthemis nobilis*) induces a restful meditative state. Representing the harmonious element of water, camomile may be used as a relaxing incense. The silver smoke will aid in removing any bad thoughts directed towards you. The soothing herb is available as a tea for sipping while you work.

Carnations (*Dianthus carophyllus*) include energetic vibrations to enhance the attributes of other herbs.

Catnip (*Nepeta cataria*) gives the power of cat magic to enhance feelings of comfort, security, love and happiness. If you share your life with a cat, let your companion lend its innate magical animal force by allowing him or her to sleep on the quilt. (This does not work with dogs or any other household animal.) Stroke Kitty gently from head to tail tip to draw his magic into your fingers before sewing or working with the quilt.

Hyacinth (*Hyacinthus orientalis*) is a feminine plant representing the planet of love, Venus, and the tranquil element of water. The fragrance of the delicate spring flower will soothe depression.

Dried lavender (*Lavendula officinale*) maintains the peacefulness of a dwelling, clears heaviness of spirit, promotes healthful sleep, draws love, heals, and protects.

Morning glories (*Ipomoea spp.*, also called bindweed in the natural state) planted in the garden or in a pot will bring peace and happiness as they open their sacred sky-blue blossoms. Morning glory is a masculine flower, under the auspices of the robust planet Saturn. However, do not include the seeds or pressed plant matter in your quilt as morning glory is poisonous. Cloth with the printed patterns of morning glories may be used.

Myrtle (*Myrtus communis*) draws universal feelings of peace. Plan a sapling near your home and nurture the bush carefully while being mindful of your purpose in planting the shrub.

What Colors Should I Select That Will Aid in My Goal of Inner Harmony?

In the harmony quilt, as well as the healing quilt, an artistically pleasing balance of colors and pattern placement is particularly important. Sharp contrasts in shapes and colors should be avoided; a gentle shading of colors is best.

Thoughtful self-examination will reveal the quality that you must augment in order to restore the harmonious balance within your life. There are corresponding colors to aid in developing the talents we desire.

Chinese practices have tied a large number of meanings to using and wearing color in order to affect our lives. Green, accented with black and white, will increase benevolence. Elements of trustworthiness are enabled by earth colors of brown, yellow, and orange. Earth tones encourage a person to be more open.

Intelligence, courtesy, and flexibility in dealing with others will be improved with the use of black and light green. Passivity will be enlivened by red, and hot tempers damped by dark green and black. Nervousness will be soothed by greens. Green, blue, black, and red enhance compassion. Patience will be increased with light blue, red, tan, and shades of earth browns.

Violet promotes thoughts of peace, harmony, and wisdom. In the aura of an individual, it indicates spirituality. Pale lilac denotes cosmic consciousness and love for humanity. Indigo blue represents the higher cognitive powers, insight, perception, and wisdom. All shades of blue bring tranquility and healing. The color blue is a charm for happiness, harmony, and joy.

The traditional color of peace, white, should be used to accent the designs.

Gray is a color/not color—a smoky, ambiguous color. In a symbolic marriage of white and black, the great opposites, a balance and resolution of conflict is signified. A silver or pewter shade, such as the sea during a storm, can give the wish of hope and fair weather after a dangerous time.

Black is the hue for protection against negative thoughts and hostility. Black represents the attributes of water in the feng shui scheme of decoration. Include black for the water qualities of peace and protection, knowledge and wisdom.

Bad luck in life is thought to be caused by disharmony in the forces of one's life energy. One way this imbalance can be remedied is with thoughtful application of color magic.

A Chinese charm for changing your luck is to wear an outfit that includes all seven colors of the spectrum. The seven-color spectrum refers to the rainbow, a symbol of nature's power and beauty. As the seven colors can appear from the white oneness of pure light, so can opposing forces be properly balanced in life. The spectrum or rainbow symbol may be used in a harmony quilt in the same fashion.

Something old,
something new,
Something borrowed,
something blue.

—Anonymous wedding
charm for good luck

How Shall I Word My Secret Wishes? Where Should I Put Them?

After a period of thoughtful meditation, compose your personal desire for harmony into a short statement. This declaration could be something like:

> "I want to become more in tune with the natural rhythms of my life. I will not fight against the forces of nature within me. I will learn to live with and benefit from my natural energy cycles."

Other desires for harmony have been worded as:

> "I wish to become more balanced in my life habits. I will not let my work or play eat up my life. I will achieve a healthful balance in my activities."

> "I desire to build a harmonious relationship in my personal life. I will not strive to be the leader or resign to be the follower. I will become an equal, reflecting the whole."

Make your statement as brief and to the point as possible. Write your decision on a sheet of clean, new white paper. I suggest preparing a cloth envelope to be used as the central focal square of the quilt. Place your written desire in the envelope. Sew or fasten the flap closed in a permanent manner to show your resolve in commitment to the goal of achieving balance and harmony in your life. Do not dilute the focus of your wish by asking for any other thing in this quilt.

What Deities May Be Petitioned for Help in My Goal?

You may wish to request the aid of one or more of these sacred beings.

Astarte: (Canaanite) Goddess representing coming together of male and female principles

Doli: (Navaho) The bluebird, a helpful deity, a symbol of peace and happiness

Irene: (Greek) Goddess of peace

Kwan-non: (Japanese) Goddess of mercy and compassion

Kuan-yin: (Chinese) Mother goddess bringing tolerance and mercy, peace and balance

Ochosi: (West Indian, African) Balances the forces of the universe; destructor of the obsolete, creator of new life; Symbol of purity and idealism; Her colors are violet, red, green and blue

Pax: (Roman) goddess of peace and reconciliation

Tara: (Chinese) goddess of mercy and compassion; eternally youthful and dressed in green

Tane: (Polynesia) god of peace and beauty

What Stones and Natural Amulets Shall I Include?

Gems are selected to produce and enhance vibrations sympathetic to your aim. They may be sewn, tied, glued, or hidden within your work in order to add vitality in empowering your goal. The stones may be placed in your "Peace Bath" opening ritual before use in the quilt. Incorporate the color of these stones in your work. A gem elixir may also be prepared to draw additional power into the artistic creation of your talisman.

Adventurine symbolizes and strengthens the awareness of peace within, self-acceptance, and calm. The stone can "draw out" old bitterness that causes disharmony within a soul.

Amber, a once-living element, radiates a deep golden warmth and helps restore the yin/yang balance vital to symmetry of self. Amber will lift depression, absorb counteractive feelings, and bring feelings of calmness.

Amethyst unlocks subconscious blocks to well-being, aids in stress relief and the banishment of fears. Known to enhance spirituality, the lavender amethyst raises the emotions, soothes the mind, and balances and increases intuitive awareness. The stone assists the regulation of healthy sleep patterns, which would help dispel bodily causes of disharmony.

Sea-green aquamarine quickens intellect and promotes clear and logical thinking. The water-like hue refreshes the quality of beneficial introspection and sharpens self-knowledge.

Cool blue or gray chalcedony is said to stimulate optimism and enhance spiritual and artistic creativity.

Yellow citrine finds among its qualities the ability to give a sense of direction to those who feel their life's path is aimless. The gem will restore feelings of self-worth and dissolve depression.

Red coral, once a living animal, adjusts attunement to nature and brings physical tranquility.

Heavy black hematite radiates all-around peace and gives a feeling of safety and protection. Hematite facilitates contemplation and meditation, refreshes and soothes.

Lapiz is known as the "Stone of Heaven." The dark blue stone dispels despondency to free the soul to regain natural balance. The gem aids acquisition of wisdom and perception of truth. It is a mental cleanser that assists in psychic development and builds mental stability. Lapis cleanses the aura and cuts through superficialities, allowing a seeking soul to find inner truth.

Velvet green malachite raises the spirits and erases mental blockages that hinder spiritual growth.

Peridot invigorates the quality of inner vision. The clear yellow-green gem opens the mind and realigns unbalanced emotional states.

Rose quartz soothes emotional trauma and restores confidence eroded by neglect. The stone will heal internal wounds caused by sorrow and bitterness. Rose quartz is a stone of love, opening the heart to love of self and love of others.

Sodalite is reassuring, protective, and cools anger. Sodalite firms courage, clears rigid thought patterns, and gives flexibility to enlarge mental perspective. This gem balances and stills the mind.

Tiger's eye's golden fire heartens clear thinking. The gem gives self-confidence and intensifies the ability to see the way through a problem if confusion or emotion cloud the issue.

Pink tourmaline promotes inner wisdom, the talent to understand your emotions and control them.

Most of these semi-precious gems and minerals are available quite inexpensively in nature stores, craft supply shops and flea markets.

Discovering a crystal digging area is an exciting experience. During a hectic and trying time of our lives, my daughter and I felt surrounded by hostile, negative thoughts. Our creative work was being stunted and blocked by ill feelings directed toward us.

We took a day trip to the Arkansas hills and spent hours picking up beautiful crystal points from the blood-red clay. As the time passed, although fatigued, we began to feel wonderfully clear-headed and energized. It was as if the mountain full of crystal was guiding a great singing beam of cleansing power through our bodies. We returned to our work feeling at peace. We were again able to dip into the reservoir of spiritual and physical energy that mental harmony brings.

If you are able to gather crystals or gems from nature, observe a few common courtesies. Ask permission from the earth and the stone itself. Tell the crystal what will be required and how you will use the points. You will know if the stone will accept or decline its use by the feeling you receive in your hand. Some describe this as a feeling of warmth and compatibility in the palm and fingers. If the crystal does not feel right, return the point to its resting place.

Say thank you by leaving an offering of silver such as a new dime or wine, or do something from your heart that will protect and enhance nature. Tidy the area of litter or plant flowers nearby.

Are There Traditional Quilt Patterns for This Kind of Quilt?

The "ocean waves" design is a traditional quilt pattern that might enhance feelings of harmony.

What Ideograms Could I Include?

Trace, photocopy, or paint a selection of the Chinese ideograms that express your desires. In historic Eastern thought, the written word was thought to hold the spiritual significance of the thought expressed, the essence of creation. Each character flows from one original brush stroke, the eternal oneness, the harmonious chord of creation. A small but excellent book containing forty characters and a short explanation of each is *The Spirit of the Chinese Character*, by Barbara Aria.

A selection of ideograms for this quilt could include: harmony, happiness, enlightenment, tranquility, and forgiveness.

Ho, the character for harmony, implies everything in proper proportion, moderation in order to achieve inner harmony. Tranquility, *an*, shows that peace comes when universal energies of heaven and earth, the dynamic tension of masculine yang force and feminine yin power, are in balance.

There are two great Asian philosophical social codes: Taoist and Confucian. Taoist philosophy taught that the balance and peaceful symmetry of life—the inner harmony—would be preserved through simplicity, by cultivating open- heartedness and acknowledging and refining the ability to cast off the false perceptions and distinctions made between people and the universe. Taoists seek seclusion and see the study of nature and its interrelations as the path to spiritual understanding.

Confucian thought points the path to inner harmony as developing "the four constant virtues"—those of propriety, wisdom, compassion, and benevolence. Proper human behavior towards one another would produce the correct balance of personal and universal life.

The ideograms for the ideals and virtues prized by these two ancient philosophies will help focus your efforts to achieve your own inner peace. Harmony within is a worthy goal that has been desired since humankind realized the potential to internalize emotions.

An is the Chinese ideogram for tranquility.

Please Suggest Some Stitching Patterns and Finishing Techniques.

After assembling the body of the quilt to your satisfaction, add the final touches that bless and energize the charm. Stitching designs similar to the quilting patterns of common quilts should be added over the surface of the fabric. The patterns and stitches will bind the fabric and your intentions together.

Words, phrases, a simple statement of the wish itself may be stitched across the fabric or along the edges. This will firmly unite your desire and your work with knot magic.

Stitching patterns should include interlocked circles, spirals, waves, and water symbols. The circle form inspires and represents harmony. Traditional Japanese sashiko stitching patterns have many simple and elegant designs representing water such as the *seigaiha*, "blue waves" or the "thousand wave" pattern. Sashiko is a technique using large, even stitches and thick thread of a contrasting color.

After completing the quilting, add any surface embellishment such as charms, extra cloth envelopes, stone amulets, or ribbons. If you intend to use your quilt as a meditation mat, add the charms around the edges so your comfort will not be disturbed by bumps and lumps.

Finish by cutting any uneven edges straight if necessary. Bind the four sides in black, to form a shield against negative thoughts.

What Aroma Shall I Add to Enhance the Intent of This Composition?

Oils of gardenia and lilac stroked on the quilt create an aura of happiness. Rose, hyacinth, and cumin fragrances bring peace.

Can You Suggest a Closing Ritual?

I've included two closing rituals to reinforce your dedication to bringing balance into your life. Select one that is compatible to your goal.

CLOSING RITUAL FOR REMEDY OF MATERIAL OR SPIRITUAL DISHARMONY

If you have decided that your disharmony is being caused by the accumulation of things—material and spiritual bad baggage—this ritual will help you let go.

Create an altar area and cover it with black cloth. The black hue is the color of chaos—the disorder that all things come from and all things return. Fold or drape your finished talisman quilt on the cloth.

Set up two black candles and charge them with focusing your intent to bring order into your life.

Place fallen leaves or wilted flowers before the candles. These things will represent the useless things you are carrying. The leaves and flowers have served their purpose and are ready to begin another cycle. Picture yourself placing on the altar all the mental refuse and debris that you are carrying.

You may wish to write a list or draw a picture of the things that you consider hindrances to your harmony and balance. Burn this list or picture in the candle flame. See yourself as preparing and cleaning yourself to begin a new cycle in your life.

Light sandalwood, myrrh, or cedar incense. Visualize the smoke carrying the burdens away from any influence on your life. This may be the time for you to meditate about what you wish to accomplish with your life. Release situations that are irritating you; let them float away and become part of the power driving the universe, turning negative into positive energy flow. Pull peace into your body with every breath.

Calmly and lovingly address your chosen goddess or god and request that the sacred one relieve you of the weight of resentments, anger, and unproductive emotions. Aim these thoughts away into the black chaos and know that your prayer is heard.

Remove the flowers and leaves from the altar. Take them outside and bury them so that they may become part of the natural cycle of life. Cast away these unnecessary things. Feel cleansed and lightened.

CLOSING RITUAL FOR INCREASING TOLERANCE

If you feel your imbalance has been influenced not by someone or something, but your reaction to it, a second closing ritual to increase your tolerance may be needed.

Aloe is a token of tranquil endurance. The plant thrives in difficult, desert-like conditions. The dark thick-leaved plant is the holy herb of Islam, symbolic of patient submission. In a region of Saudi Arabia aloe is called *saber*, meaning "patient." Aloe is planted at the edges of graves to signify patience during the wait between death and resurrection.

Aloe may be used in baths to assist the development of self-control toward abrasive people or the enlargement of tolerance toward shortcomings.

Some personalities can lacerate and puncture your psyche the way cactus thorns would pierce your fingers. Aloe is literally a healing herb for wounds and abrasions; spiritually, it will soothe your soul. Remember, aloe is for external use only.

Aloe planted at the edge of a grave signifies patience during the wait between life and resurrection.

Cut several large leaves from the outside of the aloe's rosette formation. New leaves come from the inner area, so harvest the outer blades. Wash them gently.

Chop the blades into a coarse mince. You will notice the leaves are full of a slightly sticky clear gel. Include the gel in the steeping bowl. Use ¼ to ½ cup chopped leaves. Pour 2 cups of boiling water over the minced greens and gel. Allow this mixture to steep until the water cools.

Mash the leaves into the water with the back of a silver or wooden spoon to extract as much of the juice as possible. Strain through a cheesecloth or tea strainer. Draw a warm bath for yourself and add this liquid to your bath water. As you bathe, think of the qualities of patience and serenity being enlarged within your spirit. Finish your bath with a brisk, cool shower to add energy to your resolutions.

How Shall I Use My Finished Quilt to the Best Advantage?

I use my harmony quilt as a mat to kneel on during meditation. When the quilt is not in use, I keep the composition folded over the back of my favorite chair.

If there is a particular place that seems to activate inharmonious feelings, that would be the place to display (or conceal) the talisman.

Summary

DAY TO BEGIN

Monday: Day of the Moon
Beginning of waxing or waning lunar cycle

SIGNIFICANT DATES

January 30 or June 3: Roman festival of Pax (Peace)

February 22: Concordia, Roman feast of harmony and time to make peace

May 25: Celebration of Tao, the Way to the heart

COLORS

black: protection against hostility, water qualities of peace and wisdom

black with light green: intelligence, courtesy and flexibility in dealing with others

blues: tranquility, healing, joy

brown, yellow, orange: trustworthiness

earth tones: openness

gray: a balance of conflict is resolved

green: soothes nervousness

green, blue, black and red: enhance compassion

green, accented with black and white: benevolence

dark green with black: cool hot tempers

indigo blue: higher cognitive powers

pale lilac: cosmic consciousness

rainbow: spectrum is a symbol of Nature's power to bring life into balance. A charm to change your luck.

red: dissolve passivity

silver: hope after difficult times

violet: peace, wisdom, harmony

white: peace, accent of spirituality

FABRIC MOTIFS

bats: the Five Blessings of Peace, happiness, virtue, wealth and longevity

dove: peace and universal harmony

fish: averts evil, brings wealth, married joy, harmony; symbol of perseverance

passion flowers: peace, calming of trouble

roses: love, release of personal stress, calmness

water: peace, protection

IDEOGRAMS

enlightenment

forgiveness

happiness

harmony

tranquility

STONES AND NATURAL AMULETS

adventurine: peace within, dispels bitterness

amber: restores symmetry of self

amethyst: banishes fear, unlocks blocks to creativity

aquamarine: promotes clear thinking

chalcedony: stimulates optimism and creativity

coral: physical tranquility, attunement to nature

citrine: restores feelings of self-worth, dissolves depression

hematite: peace, safety, aids contemplation, soothes

lapiz: dispels despondency, aids wisdom, mental cleanser

malachite: erases mental blockages

peridot: inner vision

rose quartz: restores confidence eroded by neglect, soothes emotional trauma

sodalite: gives courage, cools anger, gives flexibility to enlarge mental perspective

tiger's eye: gives self-confidence, improves clear thinking

tourmaline: inner wisdom, ability to control emotions

HERBS AND FLOWERS

aloe: patience, protection, peace, healing

basil: peace, love, happiness

bay leaves, cloves: ward off negativity

carnation: enhances energy of other herbs and flowers

camomile: restful meditation

catnip: adds animal magic power, enhances happiness

cumin: peace

hyacinth: Venus, water element, soothes depression

lavender: draws love, heals and protects

lilac: happiness

morning glory: peace and happiness

myrtle: peace

rose: peace, love

FRAGRANCES

gardenia, lilac: happiness

rose, hyacinth, cumin: peace

STITCHING PATTERNS

hand print: resolve to action, personal commitment

interlocked circles: strength, harmony, peace

spirals: inner serenity and magic

water symbols, waves: peace, patience, the Way of Tao

Texas Star Quilt, circa 1960. Multicolored cotton diamonds form concentric circles. Center: bright yellow multipointed star (energy, power, warmth). Second ring of color: greens (health, growth) patterned in ferns and ivy (faithfulness, health, luck, and protection). Pieces of the pattern are composed of cloth from clothes of the author, saved from early childhood until her marriage. Fabric was purchased only for the red outer setting and the central yellow star. Outer setting of star is red cotton (passion, power, energy, and courage). This quilt was made by the author, her mother, and grandmother, prior to the author's wedding.

Double Wedding Ring Pattern, circa 1937.

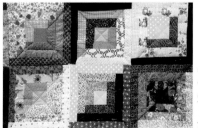

Log Cabin Pattern, circa 1996.
Blocks are "built" around the central yellow or orange "hearthstone" block in the center. One side of block is predominantly dark colored, the other side is light. Top mounted and secured to batting and plain muslin backing with pins and one line of machine stitches.

Douglas Deutscher

Talisman Quilt, circa 1997. This finished talisman incorporates many different elements that combine to create a tangible spell for love. Components include appropriate stitching patterns, embellishments, pockets filled with magical wishes, and colors with beneficial attributes. With all intentions tightly focused on a single wish, this becomes a very powerful work. The basic pattern is a modified log cabin, in which the design is enlarged so that a single square comprises the entire quilt top and provides a simple image of a happy home. The black border provides protective energies and a strong frame for the colors, designs, and accents of the interior of the quilt design and construction.

The detail photographs of this talisman on these pages focus on specific elements, with explanations for each color, pattern, and embellishment.

Douglas Deutscher

Sashiko stitching in modified shippo pattern, similar to American Wedding Ring Pattern. The eternal, repeating circles represent love and faithfulness.

This detail shows several different elements. Fabric and patterns: apples (fruit of love, Venus), roses and violets (love, beauty, kindness), denim (rejects bad thoughts and ill will). Colors: black (protection), red (passion, courage), pink (love), purple (intellect, wisdom, paired with red it represents energy of life). Embellishments (top to bottom): tiger's eye (clear thinking), orange ribbon (energy, passion), glass bead attached with ribbon has a peony design (womanly perfection, grace), ivy (fidelity), toy money (prosperity), green bird sequin (shiny sequin deflects sadness or evil thoughts; bird shape is a reference to the bride's name), shell and pearl (wisdom, Venus), calcite (improvement of physical energy), coins (prosperity), costume jewelry ring (eternity). On denim strip: bees (the virtue of work, the sweetness of life).

A simple pocket has been attached to the surface of the quilt. The lion on the fabric represents protection and strength. Tucked inside, a hand-written magical affirmation of love.

Heavy, white pearl thread and a simple running stitch were used to stitch the outline of the maker's hand. The human hand is one of the oldest and most powerful magical patterns—always remember to add yours to your creations.

Chinese ideograms *ai*, love, and *jen*, patience (not shown), have been applied to white satin. The ideograms symbolize qualities necessary for a strong relationship. In the center is a handpainted cloth valentine. White is a color of peace, satin is a fabric associated with pleasure. The pinks used encourage joy, happiness, and feelings of affection. The denim is from an old pair of the recipient's jeans.

Crazy Quilt, circa 1907. This is an antique crazy quilt (see photograph below). The squares are made of pieces of fabric left over from projects, cut from old clothing, and from other sources. Each square was then pieced together with other squares to create a full-size quilt. The pattern is easily adaptable to your own magical talisman, as the pattern allows for many colors, patterns, and stitched embellishments (such as the dog, bow, flower, and owl seen in these photographs).

Chapter 9

A Quilt for Protection

A Blanket Against Life's Slings and Arrows

He unfolds himself in the storm clouds,
He washes his mane in the blackness of the seething
* whirlpools,*
His claws are in the fork of the lightning,
His scales begin to glisten in the back of the
* rain-swept pines,*
His voice is heard in the hurricane....

—Chinese poetry

Sometimes it is impossible not to feel that the stress and abrasions of everyday life are not directed toward us personally. Attitudes of the people around us can strike as surely and as painfully as arrows. Having a personal talisman of protection can help you feel defended from the venom of jealousy, the turn of luck that seems particularly malignant, the bad feelings that can suck joy from your life like the legendary Nosferatu.

What Is a Protection Quilt Used For?

Wrap this quilt around you and picture yourself shielded and renewed for the fight. Your talisman could be draped at the head or foot of your bed, or hung as a wallhanging in the area where you spend the most time. It is also possible to construct the quilt, cut the blanket up before binding the edges and sew the flat cloth into a simple vest before adding amulets and embellishments.

Remember, however, that a quilt constructed in the magical manner is not to be washed.

How May I Begin to Bring a Feeling of Peace and Safety To My Environment?

Fear is a dog with a loud bark. Fright can rage at us from many places, trying to spread rabid hysteria wherever anxiety can find a receptive mind. Noise surrounds us like the prickly hedge that grew around the fairytale castles, spreading thorns and hate. Begin to cultivate silence. Seek contemplative, harmonic sounds whenever you can. Listening to calming instrumental music, particularly music with the rhythm of the sea and sounds of nature, will aid your task.

I have chosen to be at peace. The elimination and resolution of any kind of conflict in my environment is vital to my well-being and feelings of energy. While I am doing any magic project or task that involves creativity, I do not watch television or listen to popular or rock music, or have it on in the background. I cherish music that inspires my spiritual work, and have found it is best not to use music with lyrics as the words will distract my childlike subconscious from the purpose. I have refused to let the television step into my house and take it over with the disharmony and greed that I am trying to banish from my mind and environment. Perhaps an environmental modification such as limiting your hours of television viewing or choice of background music will enhance your feelings of security and well-being.

Create in your mind a picture of yourself in a safe, calm space. Make a physical effort to construct such a space, even in some small matter as controlling the noise or light of your area. Discord has no place there. Reassert your control.

How Long Will It Take to Make a Protection Quilt?

Although you may be tempted to hurry, do not rush through any steps of this project. It will most likely take one lunar cycle, about thirty days, to complete this quilt.

When Is the Best Time to Start Work on a Magic Quilt for Protection?

Projects involving simple spells for protection should be done in the period of time that the Moon is waxing. The growing of the lunar disc symbolizes the growing and increase of your confidence and security.

If you examine your feelings closely about the source of your ill-feelings, you may wish to fine-tune the "birth-time" of your project. A time coinciding with the waxing Moon is used to gain or increase safety, protection, constructive emotions and good fortune. The waning or decreasing Moon is used to banish bad influences, danger, loneliness, negative feelings, and bad luck.

Tuesday, the day of Mars, is the weekday to begin a protective spell. The energies of Mars are called upon for physical defense, courage, banishing evil, and vanquishing an enemy's power. Beginning the activity during a thunderstorm would be ideal in order to add energy. Working in a thunderstorm is likely to attract the attention of your personal power dragons. (Lightning strikes may be attracted, so take sensible safety precautions.) The month of October, month of the powerful primordial Goddess Hecate, is a time for spells involving protection and respectful memory of the past. The month of June is named for Juno, protector of women, and the early summer month is a beneficial time for creating a talisman that is intended to safeguard women.

January 8, is the feast day of the Roman goddess of justice, Justicia. February 12 is a day for remembrance of Diana, protector of wild things. February 16, marks the celebration of Victoria, Roman goddess of victory.

Use the power of the waxing Moon to gain safety, protection, and good fortune.

How Shall I Prepare My Workbox?

Because this workbox begins to accumulate the aura of protection you wish to build, select a box that is strong and sturdy. A chest of stout wood such as oak would be suitable, or a metal covered wooden box, such as a footlocker. Cleanse the container with sea salt and sunshine. Wrap a gold or red cord around the box and tie the rope firmly when the box is not open for use. You may wish to add a lock, either real or symbolic, to aid in your feeling of security.

How Big Should This Quilt Be?

This quilt should be of a size that will give assurance where you need it. Decide whether the construction will be of a small size, so that you can hang the fabric in your workplace and gain confidence from the sight, or if it will be large enough to wrap up in at night. Perhaps the fabric composition should be small enough to fold up and carry in your pocket. Decide what would be best to enhance your perception of protection.

What Materials Are Needed?

A quilt for protection and security will require you to select fabric, designs, stones, herbs, and small items that carry the traditional powers of protection. This chapter will explain and list materials appropriate to this purpose. You will need candles, a workbox, sharp scissors, needles, sewing thread, pearl cotton thread, batting, and cloth for backing. When you empower your selected cloth, use pure water, non-metallic pots, a new wooden spoon, salt, and herbs.

How Shall I Construct My Beginning Dedication Ritual? What Shall I Meditate or Concentrate on as I Work?

Use incense and meditation to increase a quality of security. The following is a meditation I frequently use and a suggested incense.

Using a calendar giving the lunar phases, find the seven nights before the Moon begins its increase. A wish made in the waning Moon serves to take away or diminish, as the Moon diminishes in apparent size. See the wish carried by this fragrant incense neutralizing the negativity and hostility around you.

PROTECTION MEDITATION INCENSE

    2   parts sandalwood
    1   part bay
    1   part rosemary

For each of the seven nights, smolder the incense near an open window. As the incense does its work, read inspirational and spiritually uplifting books. If you have a favorite text, read several pages to soothe and center yourself before resuming construction of your talisman each day. Work with will and concentration to build an inner dialogue with your emotions and the bodily reactions they produce. Knowledge gives control.

To use incense to augment visualization, burn incense with a component of cloves. This will drive away hostile forces and stop gossip. The odor of cloves produces high spiritual vibrations to aid your concentration.

In work to produce protection, many of the qualities that are necessary in developing personal harmony are called upon. Look within yourself to find those strengths that are needed; they will be there.

For a protection ritual and to cancel negative forces, you can perform the following before you have cut the cloth for the quilt sections.

Wear an amber, yellow topaz, or red coral amulet or jewelry with these stones if you have such pieces. Hold a black candle between your palms. State your wish clearly in a simple way, such as:

> "I want the feelings of unkindness I feel around me to return to their source."

> "All negative forces near me will be canceled."

> "My personal aura of strength and invulnerability will be augmented."

The black candle may be dressed with Spell Weaver Oil, made up of equal parts of sandalwood and lily oil. Light the black candle, which is now charged with removing any negativity directed toward you. Picture any aggressive ill-will being burned up by the candle flame and deflected by the light. Place the candle before a round mirror so that the flame is reflected.

Light a white candle in another part of the room where the image will not be reflected in the mirror. Let both these candles burn completely out rather than physically extinguishing them.

When doing any magic with candles, be sure they are in a safe place, not near blowing curtains or where a child or pet could knock over the tapers. If you have a fireplace, the candle can be burned inside the hearth. Use practical candle holders that prevent fire hazards and do not allow the wax to stain or run on your table.

After both candles have been lit, arrange your fabric, amulets, herbs, thread, and other objects near the black candle and mirror so that the glow of candlelight touches the articles. Spread your hands over the fabric and amulets. Press the cloth and items with your palms. Feel strength and love enter your materials. Picture any bad feelings returning to their source, vaporized in the candle flames and turned away from you.

Do not visualize harm or mischief occurring to the thing or person responsible for the disharmony in your life. Simply returning the energy from whence it came is appropriate. My personal mental projection in this exercise is of a group of tattered black birds flying away in a disorderly flock, or cobwebs and rags being burned in the candle flame. I picture black thoughts that look like dark arrows striking the flame and being repelled. Sometimes the picture of an electric bug zapper comes to my mind—each bad thought hits the energy field and dies with a fine electric sizzle.

What Cloth and Designs Will Strengthen My Talisman for Protection?

New cloth is best for most of this quilt. Use fabric patterns with red geraniums, violets, stars, circles, mistletoe, ferns, tomatoes, tulips, periwinkles, onions, mirrors, or pictures of things representing strength and security to you. Perhaps lions, a geometric stone wall, dinosaurs, the Power Rangers, dragons, or even thorny roses will provide that feeling. The image of such an object will bring the symbolic essence to your mind.

Fabric from your own garments may be used for the inner parts of the design, but should be bordered and shielded by new, strong cloth.

There is a process for easily transferring photos to fabric. Simple kits can be purchased at craft shops that reproduce the photographic image on your cloth without damaging the original photo. Many copy shops, such as Kinko's, can also duplicate your original document on cloth. Using a fabric-photo of yourself as the central hearth square of the Log Cabin pattern makes an effective central motif for a protective quilt talisman. These fabric-photos are useful in any of the magic quilts to personalize and focus the thought being produced in the work.

Another motif to keep in mind are dragons. The Eastern Dragon is the symbol of a good guardian, full of the active forces of nature. The Wise Father Dragon had nine good sons; they are found protecting various things. The River Dragon watches rivers and bridges. The Fighter Dragon is the sentinel of swords. You and your household are eternally watched over by a personal smaller dragon.

The five-clawed dragon of the East is a wise, beloved creature. Sometimes he is painted with a precious pearl, the Pearl of Wisdom, in his talons. Above all, he seeks wisdom, and is the embodiment of power, goodness, and life force.

The dragons of the West, such as in English folklore, are often villainous, tricky, and above all covetous of things that they cannot use. Why does the wicked dragon prowl to keep the lovely virgin imprisoned? The serpent cannot benefit from the pure girl in any way, but covets her so that no one else may claim her love. For your purposes, cultivate the wisdom and force of the Eastern Dragon.

Dragons are fond of black tea. If you drink a china cup full of steaming Oolong as you meditate over your handwork sometimes it is possible to lure your personal dragon into sight—but only if the wise beast is willing.

Add images of Asian dragons to your talisman. Reward their vigilance by sewing pearls near them.

What Herbs and Plants Should Be Used for Empowerment and Inclusion?

Use leaves, sprigs, twigs, or small pinches of the following herbs behind the patches or in the pockets of the quilt: ash tree leaves, basil, dill, fern, mistletoe, rose geranium, rosemary, rowan, tarragon, or black pepper. Of these, ash leaves (*Fraxinus excelsior*), mistletoe (*Viscum album*) and rowan (*Sorbus acuparia*) are most strong in guardian protective powers.

Basil (*Ocimum basilicum*) is used in the rainforest to ward off evil and to break bad habits. Basil is under the planetary influence of Mars and has the affections of the deities Vishnu and Erzulie. European traditional magic uses basil in exorcism incenses and purification baths. A basil plant in the house brings protection.

Black pepper, mixed with equal portions of the mineral sea salt, should be spread liberally between the layers of cloth for this talisman. Pepper is under the shield of Mars; it neutralizes corruptive and foul energies and frees the mind of envious thoughts.

Copal (*Bursera odorata*) incense is burned in the jungles and in Mexico to protect against negative magic and spiritual malaise such as envy and grief. Rosemary (*Rosemarinus officinalis*) may be added to the incense to raise a barrier against envy and unpleasantness.

Mistletoe is sacred to the deities of Apollo, Venus, Freya, Odin, and Frigga. The saprophyte has long been used for protection against lightning, disease, and evil of general natures. Caution: mistletoe is poisonous; use care in handling. Cloth printed with the images of these flowers and plants may be used, instead.

Peony (*Paeonia officinalis*) represents the "ideal of femininity" in Asian art, but in European magic this lush flower is a follower of the masculine Sun and emblem of the element of Fire. If the plant or its image is worn, powerful guardianship of spirit and body is given. Planted near the home or kept in a room, the peony shelters against vileness. Parts of the plant to be used in a charm should be gathered at night.

Special care should be taken not to step on peony seeds, as it is said that this will promote a quarrel with the very person you should most avoid. Scattered seeds sow disorder and strife, but the root may be used in a charm to reverse bad thoughts sent against the person holding the amulet.

Periwinkle (*Vinca minor*) is a powerful magical herb, but the plant and blossoms are poisonous and must be gathered according to a certain protocol in order to be efficacious. Fabric with the image of the multi-colored periwinkle would be best for your use. Pots or flowerbeds full of the easily grown flowers are beneficial for screening against vagrant bad spirits and the sending of malignant thoughts toward you.

Tomatoes (*Lycopersicon spp.*) are under the feminine auspices of the planet Venus. The plants in the garden, shiny red fruit and yellow flowers, ward against malevolence. A pot of patio tomatoes on your porch can work double duty, being a guardian as well as a tasty salad ingredient.

Tulips (*Tulipa spp.*) are charms for protection and prosperity. Many fabrics with a print of multicolored tulips are available in the spring.

Cloth may be steeped with rosemary leaves or sprigs to increase defensive energies. Rosemary is easily grown in pots to be kept near the door of your house. This herb is one of the oldest incenses and when burned, rosemary emits powerful cleansing and purifying vibrations. It is smoldered to rid a place of negativity, especially prior to performing magic.

"When placed beneath the pillow, rosemary ensures good sleep and drives away nightmares. Laid under the bed, sprigs protect the sleeper from all harm. Rosemary is also hung on the porch and doorposts to keep thieves from the house..." (*Cunningham's Encyclopedia of Magical Herbs*, Llewellyn, 1993).

Include herbs in combinations of three, seven, or nine. Pictures of these plants can also be placed in pockets or sewn on the body of the work.

How Shall I Prepare and Empower My Cloth?

For more general details about charging cloth, please refer to the original explanation in Chapter One.

There are several options for obtaining pure, energetic water for use in empowering your supplies. You can collect rainwater to use for charging your cloth or preparing gem elixirs, or draw well water on a sunny day at noon, when the Sun is at its peak. Pure bottled spring water or sea water collected at the beach are good choices, as well.

Fill an enamel or glass vessel with the water. Add a double handful of sea salt to the cold water. Measure with your hands, not a cup. Hold the salt tightly in your fist and swirl in a clockwise motion until the salt is dissolved. Picture your problems melting as the salt does. Next, add three generous pinches each of three of the following herbs: basil, dill, rose geranium leaves or blossoms, rosemary, tarragon, cloves. Add a large pinch of black pepper. Think of the fragrance surrounding you with an aura of love and reassurance of safety.

Continue to stir gently with a new wooden spoon. Slowly bring the water to a boil. Allow the water to simmer for three, seven, or nine minutes.

Allow the water to cool. Wet the fabric and place the cloth you are to use for this quilt in the infused water. Lift the cloth up and down several times using the wooden spoon and make certain that the cloth is saturated. Let it steep overnight. If possible, place the pot outside in the moonlight, taking care to protect it from animals and children.

The next day, rinse the fabric well to eliminate any possible irritation from the herbs and salt. Allow the cloth to dry in the strong sunlight before using. Press the fabric carefully before folding it into your clean workbox. After construction is completed, the quilt should not be washed.

What Colors Will Provide an Aura of Protection?

Dark indigo blue rejects bad thoughts being sent from someone wishing you ill. Bind or border your quilt in this color. A fabric dyed with real indigo, such as denim, would be perfect.

Colors for energy, shades of red and touches of yellow, and spiritually uplifting hues of violet and purple should be used. Include the color saffron to represent the qualities of Mars. Gold lamé can also be a dramatic accent in fabric art.

Pure white should be included for the aura of security and peace it provides. An inner border of black will absorb and neutralize negativity.

Where Shall I Place Written Secret Intentions and Charms?

Amulets, charms, and written intentions may be placed between the layers of cloth or in pockets included in the seams. Cloth envelopes can be constructed and sewn to the front or back of the quilt.

What Heavenly Entities May Be Enlisted in My Search for Protection?

Diana: (Greek) protectress of wild things

Mary: (European, Judaeo-Christian traditions) compassionate protector of all who petition her

Netekwo: (Ghanaian) dark god who counteracts bad witchcraft

Nike: (Greek) fair goddess of victory in competition

Osain: (West Indian, African) represents the forces of nature; protects the house and overcomes enemies; protection of chemists, herbalists, and botanists

Oggun: (West Indies, African) protects against accidents and surgery; protects policemen, farmers, and engineers

Rolo: (Polynesian) virile god who counteracts sorcery and casts out evil spirits

Saint Anthony, Saint Joseph: victory over enemies, protection of the home

Saint Cosme, Saint Damien: protectors of children, childhood

Sekhmet: (Egyptian) lion-headed goddess of war and protection

Yemaya: (West Indian, African) rules all connected to the sea; protection against drowning and accidents on the water

What Amulets, Embellishments, and Stones Are Used For Protection?

Neither plant, jewel, nor color, the mineral salt is the one essential inclusion for any talisman for protection. This quilt should also have one or more small mirrors or large sequins attached. The mirrors symbolize the deflection of sadness and ill will.

Amulets made of strong metal, most importantly iron, should be attached. A bent iron nail is a traditional protective talisman, as is an iron horseshoe or iron or silver crucifix. Bits of gold, to recall the energy and protection of the Sun, may be sewn in.

Jewels and stones noted for their defensive qualities are yellow topaz, which banishes fears; red coral, which averts physical violence and gives psychic protection. Amber, lava, garnet, and carnelian may also be used.

Quartz crystals that have been carried by you or the person that you are shielding—but by no one else—add energy to the quilt. Before incorporating the crystals into the design, let them heat and bask in full sunlight for several days. Sew the stones between layers of cloth or in hidden pockets.

Turquoise defends against harmful experiences and attracts beneficial friendships. Green and blue turquoise has been a sacred stone since before the times of the Egyptian dynasties. In ancient Persia, turquoise was used as a powerful amulet on valuable horses to protect both them and their rider from falls and accidents. The Persians have a folk saying: "to escape evil and attain good fortune, one must see the reflection of the new moon on either the face of a friend, on a copy of the Koran, or on a turquoise." Turquoise is a sacred stone to several tribes of American Indians as well. Often turquoise was worked into pendants and amulets representing a totem animal, and used as a burial offering.

Golden tiger's eye releases tension, pulls in good luck, and averts evil. Warm, honey-colored amber is calming and will absorb negative energies, break spells, and lift depression. Midnight black jet protects from violence and dissolves depression.

If worn as a piece of jewelry, jade gives protection from enemies. It is thought that the wearer will absorb some of the virtues of the stone. Jade is a particular favorite of the Chinese culture. A variety having a rich emerald green tone is called *feits'ui*, "Kingfisher plumes," and is very rare and costly. The original ideograph *pao*, meaning *precious*, incorporates the symbols for jade beads hidden in a jar. The oldest ideographic character for king appears to be three linked dots, denoting a string of jade beads.

Jade was used as a protective talisman stone by the ancient Egyptians, Aztecs, and Maori. Maori *punamu* jade was so rare and prized that only a powerful wizard with trance-seeing abilities could locate such a stone. A stone located in such a manner was given the name of the man who found it and the piece was greatly prized as a family totem. As the male leaders of the clan wore and passed on the jade *hei-tiki*, it was believed to communicate an aura of the succession of wearers to the present owner. If the family line was dying, the last male would be buried with the charm, so that no stranger would be able to take possession of the precious stone's qualities.

A star sapphire, carrying within the heart of the jewel a living star, wards off ill luck and serves as security against destructive thoughts aimed toward the owner.

Release tension and attract good luck with golden tiger's eye.

Dark red sard is a protection against evil incantations and sharpens the wits of the one who possesses the stone. The blood hue of sard is thought to neutralize any malignant influence of black onyx, dispelling bad dreams and melancholy.

If bad snakes and aggressive wildlife are dangers, translucent green jasper has an ancient history of bringing defense against venomous snakes and driving away bad earth spirits.

Weighty black hematite, dark as a judicial robe, has the unique quality of procuring favorable decisions in lawsuits and fortunate issues involving judgments. If the stone shows a red streak within the black, it has the further ability to "confer invulnerability upon the field of battle."

Satiny American gypsum, if bought at Niagara Falls, is known as a "luck stone." Yellow Egyptian gypsum is cut into an egg form and called "Pharaoh's eye," conferring qualities of security and bringing good fortune.

An ancient Egyptian amulet for protection is an image of the sacred beetle, the scarab. Scarab charms are often found made of jade, blue glazed pottery, black stone, or silver.

Secondhand shops that carry old jewelry are often good sources for useful semiprecious stones such as coral. However, these stones should be washed carefully and cleansed in charged water in the same manner that cloth is prepared since there is often lingering sadness in old stones. If you have any doubts about a piece, it is better to use a new stone.

Bead shops, sewing supply outlets, and craft stores have small amulets, buttons, beads, and charms of inexpensive real semiprecious stones and metal. Do not use plastic, except for representations of large objects, such as a horse or car. Oriental shops also have beautiful and inexpensive small charms of metal, jade, and other semiprecious stones. Rock shops and nature stores are also good sources of crystals, stones, and shells.

Shih *is the Chinese ideogram for revelation.*

Are There Traditional Patterns for a Quilt Meant to Protect?

For experienced quilters, use a pattern such as "Boston Commons" or "Castle Walls," which could be said to represent defensive walls. A simplified "Log Cabin," one block enlarged to the complete quilt size, is easy and artistically satisfying, as well as providing the image of a central figure defended and surrounded by safety. If the "Log Cabin" pattern is used, the central hearth-square should be red, orange, or a fabric photo-processed with your picture.

What Ideograms May Be Included?

The Chinese characters for courage, wisdom, honor, revelation, peace, or forgiveness can be painted, stitched, or drawn on the cloth. The character *shih*, revelation, is composed of a stylized pictogram from ancient use showing power or light emanating from heaven, the upper world that controls nature. The character can mean "heaven sent," "an omen," or "to manifest." Shih can represent power through knowledge of what is frightening you.

Ying, courage, shows courage by the strokes for "person" standing alone in a "wilderness." He does not show fear in this wide open place.

What Stitching Patterns and Finish Shall I Use?

Use red thread to aid protective power. Quilting patterns of the magic star, tracings of your hands, concentric circles with your personal amulet or picture in the center of the radiating circles, horseshoes, the rayed Sun, and the runic symbols for protection may be stitched over this quilt.

What Fragrances Will Enhance the Intent of This Talisman?

Select one or more of the aromas of protection for your quilt. Seek to make the fragrances blend pleasurably. The mystic scent of oil of myrrh is an effective protective scent that could be stroked around this cover. Oil of bergamot may be added to the quilt or stroked lightly on your hands while working, to add its shielding aura. Bergamot is very intense—use caution when handling.

Gardenia and cypress oil offer defensive energies. Oil of rose geranium safeguards and imparts courage. You may wish to plant several rose geraniums near the doors of your house—the leaves of this plant may be used in cooking and sachet making.

Oil of petitgrain is an obscure but traditional essential oil often used in combinations for safeguarding. Petitgrain has a scent of bitter orange.

Incense components and fragrant oils can be purchased inexpensively at religious supply stores as well as at New Age shops. Small charcoal discs to use as safe bases for burning incense or smoldering essential spices are also available.

Please Suggest a Closing Ceremony.

At the completion of the magic quilt for protection, assemble and burn the following incense:

3   parts frankincense
3   parts copal
2   parts myrrh
1   part sandalwood

Leave your windows open and encourage the fresh air to sweep through as this incense burns. If the house seems full of sadness, depression, fear, or anger, the fragrance will "clear the air" for more positive thoughts. As the incense burns, collect all the garbage and trash in your house. Discard the debris away from your home while reaffirming your vow to order your life in harmony and courage, without fear.

Please Give Me Suggestions as to the Use and Display of the Finished Project.

You may wish to display your talisman for protection in the area where you feel most vulnerable in your home, office, or car. You may feel more secure to keep the quilt within its workbox container and keep the container in or near the threatening area. You may feel most comforted by spreading the quilt over your bed at night or hanging the composition at the head of your bed. I suggest keeping the quilt in a place where you can easily touch to see the protective colors and know the hidden powers within.

Summary

DAY TO BEGIN
Tuesday

COLORS
black: repels negativity

gold: energy and protection of the Sun

indigo blue: rejects bad thoughts, physical protection

red, yellow: energy, power

saffron: the color of the god Mars

white: security, peace

FABRIC MOTIFS

ferns, tomato, tulips, periwinkles, onion, garlic, mirrors: protection, ability to repel evil or harm

mistletoe: Druidic symbol of protection

red geraniums: protection from evil spells

stars, circles: ancient emblems of protection

violets: protection

IDEOGRAMS

courage

forgiveness

honor

peace

revelation

wisdom

STONES AND NATURAL AMULETS

amber: neutralizes negative energies, breaks bad spells, lifts depression

coral: averts physical violence, psychic protection

gypsum: luck, security, good fortune

hematite: aids in procuring favorable judicial decisions

iron: ancient talisman of protection and strength

jasper: defends against harmful wildlife

jade: protection from enemies

jet: protection from violence

mirrors: deflection of sadness and ill will

pearl: wisdom

quartz: energy multiplier

salt: strong protection

sard: protects against evil incantations, sharpens the wits

silver: protection from occult evil

star sapphire: security against destructive thoughts

tiger's eye: release of tension, averts evil, pulls good luck

topaz (yellow): banishes fear

turquoise: attracts beneficial friendships, guards health, defends from harm, protects from falls

HERBS AND FLOWERS

ash leaves, mistletoe, rowan: guardian protective powers, tree magic

black pepper: protection of the god Mars, neutralizes corrupt and foul energies, frees the mind of envious thoughts

cloves: drives away hostile forces, stops gossip

gardenia: protection

periwinkles: screens against vagrant bad spirits

peony: emblem of the element fire, guards body and spirit

rose geranium: courage, safeguarding

rosemary: increases defensive energy

tomatoes: protection of goddess Venus

tulips: prosperity, protection from want

FRAGRANCES:

bergamot: shielding aura

cloves: drives away hostile forces, stops gossip

cypress oil: defense

gardenia: defensive energy

myrrh: sacred protection

petitgrain: safeguarding

rosemary: increases defensive energy

rose geranium: courage, safeguarding

STITCHING PATTERNS

concentric circles: Neolithic protective symbol

horseshoe

magic star: protection from evil

outlines of maker's hands

rayed Sun

runes of protection

Chapter 10

A Quilt for Personal Energy

Achieving Inner Harmony and Balance

Each morning sees some task begun,
Each evening sees it close;
Something attempted, something done,
Has earned a night's repose.

—Henry Wadsworth Longfellow

Energy, the force that moves mountains . . . or moves us just to take a nap. It seems as if we had the energy, we could do anything. Unfortunately, the world around us is full of energy-sucking forces, like invisible tiny vampire bats, eagerly lapping at the fountain of our spiritual drive and resolution. The daily drain of necessary tasks—with the accompanying irritants of noise, abrasive personalities, and boring repetitive work—leaves us feeling mentally and physically exhausted. The loss of balance, disruption in the harmonious flow of our lifeforce, keeps us tense. As a result we tire, constantly in the alert pose like a watching Neanderthal with stick in fist, ready to fight or flee.

As you read this chapter, you will become aware that tapping the inner springs of power is a task with several components. Lassitude, lack of physical energy, often is more closely linked with mental attitude than the actual tasks we must perform. Help with inner harmony, life balance, and the free flow of the spirit within are all needed to revitalize a weary soul.

139

What Visualization or Meditation Will Help Me Bring More Energy into My Life?

Sit quietly and see yourself successfully completing a task you now consider insurmountable. Unreel the picture in your mind as clearly as if you were watching it happen. Then let the crafting of your personal beautiful talisman represent this task. Envisioning the completed quilt, a product of your ephemeral thoughts being made into a tangible object, will boost your feeling of power. Think of jobs you have completed that once you thought you could not do; remember triumphs in the past, small and large.

Choose a spot with a soothing view of nature; if you live in the city, this can be a single flower, the struggling elm near your window, even a pigeon preening on the walk. Look at the sky. Inhale deeply several times and feel the oxygen—the fuel of life—reach into every part of your body. Repeat firmly to yourself that you are a part of, and one with, the dynamic that drives nature and keeps the universe in balance.

The east wall of your home represents the energy force of your health—display green plants here.

How Shall I Bring Fresh Energy into My Environment?

Ch'i is the Chinese character for "energy," but the strokes of the ideogram are more literally and philosophically interpreted as "vitality," a unifying principle of universal energy. Ch'i circulates throughout the earth, atmosphere, and animal life—including humanity. Harmonizing your life with nature and producing an environment for yourself that is balanced and serene will enable you to participate in the fullness of energy available.

Study and follow the general principles of feng shui to make the currents of energy flowing within your living area beneficial. A simple and effective feng shui method of gaining harmonious force is the use of green plants to conduct good ch'i of a nourishing nature around your space. Green is the symbolic color of wood and trees, creating a psychic root of stability. The green plants create an aura of relaxation and restful connection with nature.

The east wall of your main room or house is thought to represent the energy force of your health. Give this area vitality by using or displaying wooden objects and green plants, especially in groups of three.

Mirrors stimulate energy flow within an enclosure. If you have difficulty with this concept, picture the dancing points of light in a twirling mirror ball as sparks of energy dart about. Do not, however, place mirrors in the bedroom as shiny objects negate the feeling of calm and restfulness you wish to engender there.

Visualize all the organs of your body working in synchronism, producing the wonder of life force that guides your hands and thoughts as you work. Feel the warmth of the colors of the Sun flow through your skin and into your life.

As you work on an energy quilt for someone else, picture the benefits for them, surrounding and infusing them. See them surrounded with healing white light.

What Is an Energy Quilt Used For?

Universally, the symbolic language of the mind is used to activate the tremendous, infinite source of cosmic power. The signs and symbols of magic act as shields to repel evil and as magnets to attract the good, beneficial qualities of spiritual forces. Your magic energy talisman will help you to release your internal potency with the knowledge and use of nature's wisdom in action using the force of your own mind.

How Long Will It Take to Make an Energy Quilt?

Perhaps you think that if you have lots of energy it wouldn't take too long to make this quilt, or if you don't have any energy at all you could take much, much longer. This is not so. Try to keep the period of time to produce your talisman at about a lunar month—28 to 30 days.

Often, a lack of energy is a reflection of a feeling of lack of control over your life. This decision to construct an energy quilt is an event you can control. When you complete your decision successfully, a bit of your psychic energy is sparked into life, fanned from a fading ember into a struggling flame that only you can feel and feed.

How Shall I Prepare My Workbox?

Supplies should be stored in a box with a top or lid and kept closed when not in use. While your work is unfinished, think of the composition and the materials you are using as chemicals ready for assembly into your personal power source. Prevent negative vibrations from attacking or inhabiting the unfinished quilt.

An energy quilt needs lots and lots of positive power! To cleanse a container to use for your workbox, sprinkle two generous handfuls of sea salt into the box and briskly dust the salt around the receptacle.

The open box and salt should bask in full sunlight for three days. Close the carton at night unless there is a full Moon—in that case, keep the box in the moonlight as well. Think of soaking up your supply of all the cosmic power available. After three days have passed, turn the container upside down over a clean sheet of white paper and tap the bottom to remove the used salt. As you do this, hold a mental picture of worn-out dead batteries falling away from you and your workbox. Close the box.

Fold the paper carefully to enclose all the salt grains that represent any energy-draining forces that have been around you. Bury or burn the paper and salt in an area away from your house.

Your workbox is now cleaned and prepared for the project in progress, or for safe storage of the finished talisman. If possible, store your workbox beneath your bed when you are not working on the energy quilt.

What Day Shall I Begin?

You should begin your energy quilt on a Sunday, the day sacred to the power of the Spiritual and to that of the Sun, which lends power and a quality of spiritual attainment. After assembling the cloth and embellishments for your quilt, lay them in the sunshine and let them become warm with the immeasurable power of a combusting star before you begin your work.

The energy quilt may also be begun on a Tuesday, the day of Mars. Mars gives masculine force useful for developing courage and physical strength.

March 21 is the day of the Spring Equinox. The day is one of celebration of all the powers in nature awakening. The blessing and happiness of Demeter is given on this day.

A day of the year not to begin an energy quilt would be Samhain (October 30) as this day commemorates the turn of the life wheel into the dark underworld.

Should I Use Special Patterns or Materials?

As with all the magic quilts, you may use a simple pattern composed of cloth from items of personal clothing, new fabric in meaningful designs and colors, personally significant embellishments, talismans, and herbs hidden in pockets or between the layers of fabric. Traditional antique quilt designs of stars would be very powerful if you wish to use them.

You will need new cloth for backing, batting in the same size you've chosen to make your talisman, safety and straight pins, needles, scissors, and thread. I also like to use a thimble to protect my fingers when stitching and quilting.

Shall I Use a Beginning Ritual to Dedicate My Work?

Prepare yourself by taking a vitalizing bath. Gather the following ingredients:

3 parts carnation
(3 drops carnation oil or
3 tablespoons dried red carnation petals)
2 parts lavender
(2 drops lavender oil or
2 tablespoons dried lavender flowers and leaves)
2 parts rosemary
(2 large sprigs of fresh rosemary or
two pinches of dried rosemary)
2 parts basil
(2 large sprigs of fresh basil or
two pinches of dried basil)

*Think of unusual motifs
to signify power—try
bulldozers, dinosaurs,
or trucks!*

Knot the herbs into a loosely woven yellow cloth or regular yellow washcloth. Before dropping the herbal bag into the bath, roll the cloth between your palms to crush the leaves and release the fragrances.

Draw a hot bath and drop the bag of energy-giving herbs into the water. Allow it to steep for three minutes. Test the water and cool it if necessary to a comfortable temperature. Step in and immerse yourself as fully as possible and visualize the water sparkling over your body, each drop giving vitality to melt and absorb into your body. Feel your fatigue and depression melt away into the water. Let your batteries charge.

Pull the plug and watch the water go down the drain. Imagine as strongly as possible that you are seeing the dregs of all the day's troubles swirling away. Take a quick, cool shower and dry off vigorously with a yellow, red, or orange towel. Breathe deeply, taking in the friendly energy of the Air spirits around you.

Untie the herb-filled cloth and picture the cells and springs of power within your body unlocked in the same way that you are unknotting the cloth. Discard the used herbs and flowers in the outdoors in order to return them to the earth.

If you do not have a bathtub, use the herb-cloth to scrub over your body as you shower. Do not sprinkle loose herbs and flowers into the water. Your feelings of peace and tranquility will be destroyed if you must pick leaves and blossoms off your wet body and out of the plumbing.

What Designs and Motifs Confer and Symbolize Power?

Select cloth with the motifs of the Sun, stars, flames, chili peppers, bamboo, and carnation flowers. The children's section of a fabric store often offers a wide range of interesting patterns. Unusual designs such as trucks or bulldozers, dinosaurs, lightning, and other motifs—even the Energizer Bunny—that would represent power and energy can be found.

Bamboo (*Bambusa vulgaris*) represents resilient strength, natural grace, and the ability to flourish under adverse conditions. A motif used for centuries in the Orient, bamboo is a symbol of survival, integrity, and fortitude.

Carnations (*Dianthus caryophyllus*), once called *gillyflowers*, are ruled by the Sun and represent the energetic element of fire. Vivid red carnations, with their characteristic piquant fragrance, can be kept in the home or workplace to remind you of your inner potential. As you pass the flowers, inhale deeply, taking in the power of the air itself. Touch the cool blossoms to remind you of your goal to balance and energize your life. The sight and touch will help you release the potency that lies sleeping within you.

Dried carnation flowers are used in power incenses. If you wish to add the intense vibration of a Sun-ruled plant to your work, prepare a power incense as follows. Burn the incense as you construct your quilt, or hide the dried and anointed petals within the quilt.

Dry nine red carnations in full Sun, where fresh air can circulate over the blossoms—good air flow is important so that the life-laden blossoms do not mold. Turn the flowers frequently and allow them to desiccate until the petals will crumble easily. It may be necessary to put the flowers in the oven at night so that they do not become wet with dew or absorb humidity. Do not heat the flowers, just allow the blossoms to dry gently with the pilot light of the oven.

On the ninth day, separate flowers from stems—you will use only the blossom. Pour one teaspoon carnation oil over the blossoms and stir gently with the fingers of your right hand until all petals are evenly anointed with the oil. As you stir, visualize the force of the Sun warming you and filling your spirit with vitality. Smolder a pinch of this high-voltage incense on charcoal when you need a lift—I stroke the essential oil of red carnations on my wrists and over my heart on days that I know I will need an extra measure of energy.

Sun, stars, and flames represent life-giving heat, light to illuminate our lives, and the transforming power of combustion. Chili peppers are the plant-world equivalent of heat and flames.

What Plants and Herbs May I Include for Energy?

For energy the following substances would be included within the quilt: ginger, mullein, vanilla, and rosemary. Other herbs to consider using are in the following list.

Artemisa (*Artemisia vulgaris*, also known as mugwort) is a feminine plant, in the element of earth and sacred to Diana and Artemis. When worn, the silver-gray plant offers physical endurance for hikes, running, or long walks. Artemisa has a sage-like smell and dries well. Europeans once stuffed pillows with the plant in order to enhance the vividness of happy dreams. A tall plant, artemisa can be grown as an ornamental, or found in the wild in waste places and ditches.

Black tea leaves should be included in talismans intended to give courage and strength. If the quilt gets wet or damp, hidden leaves may produce a stain on light-colored fabrics. An alternative method is to steep fabric in a hot, strongly brewed infusion of tea. This will change the tint of light-colored cloth somewhat. Remove the leaves before submerging the cloth into the brew or small tea-leaf stains will occur. Tea will lure your personal dragons to give you help they are fond of the steam rising from the china tea cup. Sip a cup if you like, or have one near you while you work.

Masterwort (*Imperatoria ostruthium*) is a plant embodying the masculine element of fire and is dedicated to Mars. The herb gives physical stamina if worn and firms the will.

Olives (*Olea europaea*)—leaves, pits, and oil—are sacred to Athena, Apollo, Ra, and Minerva. The cosmic vibration of the olive tree, dedicated to the Sun, spreads peace and protection.

Thistle (*Carduus spp.*), included in full or part, aids in bodily vigor and protects against evil. The hardy thistle grows under the auspices of the masculine planet Mars.

Thyme (*Thymus vulgaris*), the common cooking herb, is useful for the attraction of good health and enhancement of courage and psychic powers. Thyme is a robust, easily grown small shrub with oval gray-green leaves; it grows with the blessings of the planet Venus. The herb has powers of granting and attracting good health, courage, healing, and purification. Bees love thyme, so be careful of busy insects if you harvest your thyme from the bush.

In addition to these plants and herbs, consider using the image of dried pods of the lively chili pepper to add the element of fire and energy of heat. Or, use buttons, beads, or twigs of ebony and oak wood to symbolize the qualities of the almost eternal materials.

As a practical note, if you are using freshly picked herbs, press them overnight or for several days between layers of absorbent paper under a weight. Pressing in this manner will remove moisture. If not well dried, particularly juicy leaves or blossoms will stain fabric and can promote mildew and mold within the quilt. An allergy attack from your talisman would not be pleasant or energizing.

In drying, I flatten the leaves with my fingers on plain white paper towels, then put several layers of tissue or newsprint on top and underneath the plant matter. I use a stack of heavy books for a solid weight. Wrapping the bottom book with plastic or waxed wrap so no moisture creeps up and stains the book cover is a good idea.

Herbs may also be hung and air-dried in the traditional manner used for cooking herbs. Flowers may be dessicated by air-drying or using drying powder.

Please Suggest Some Colors to Give Me and My Quilt Energy.

Orange, gold, and its near brother, yellow, are important energy and power colors. Orange gives the high voltage of the Sun, but can stir elements of pride and bodily appetites. Orange can intensify emotions, so use it carefully.

Flame red shows strength of will and heat of vitality. Crimson red gives happiness and strength. Red in any shade can be called the symbolic color of the source of life for the universe, solar power, the pulse-color of the Sun. Radiant crimson is a way of showing the expulsion of the forces of bad energy in your body, such as the destructiveness of hate or greed. Balance red, yellow, and orange with the purity of white, to harness the horsepower of Sun colors for harmonious good.

Yellow is associated with matters of the intellect, such as learning, self-confidence, and feelings of personal power. Yellow was the color of the Imperial Emperor of China, a power color of the highest rank. This bright shade is so associated with the imperial house, that the entrance to the palace is commonly known as "the Yellow Door."

Yellow with indigo blue increases psychic well-being, boosts self-confidence, and protects from negativity. Yellow can relieve exhaustion—both mental and physical—and gives a more intellectual dynamic than orange. But be warned—yellow is an active, almost mischievous color, and it can be used for mood elevation, but not for promoting sleep.

Touches of violet and purple will balance the physical effect of the warm colors with the cool spiritual. Tan represents a successful new beginning.

That greedy energy-eater, chronic depression, is said to be helped by wearing or using apple green or purple-red. Either color will brighten your outlook. Green is healing and aids in acquiring wealth, insight, and happiness. Each of these qualities increases the life energy level. The color of hope, benevolence, and the season of spring, fresh green improves athletic coordination. A large dose of green can improve your mental and physical outlook, so use nature's color with a liberal hand.

What Saints or Deities Can Be Petitioned for Help in This Endeavor?

Of course, all the deities have power and energy. There are some that may appeal to you more than others, and if you feel a connection, address your work to that god or goddess.

Mars is a god embodying energy and power, high masculine vibrations. Mars develops courage and physical prowess.

The goddess Kundalini of India and Tibet is the Goddess of Coiled Energy and presides over the hidden fountain of life force.

What Stones, Minerals, or Other Natural Amulets Can I Add?

Include items associated with the element of fire and heat, such as brass, gold, lava, quartz crystal, and jasper.

The powers associated with fire infer that something will be changed and consumed. As a chemical reaction creates flames, the fuel is transformed into gas and heat. See your depression or inactivity transformed and changed into an energetic, productive life.

Agate improves natural vitality. The stone increases self-confidence and gives an aura of sureness to those facing any kind of test or who must call upon a sudden burst of physical or mental stamina. In general, agate gives courage and banishes fear; it balances the emotions and calms body and mind.

Amber, the tears of the Sun, lifts depression in order to free mental forces. This mysterious golden stone is a natural substance of petrified tree-sap; amber promotes calm. Amber absorbs and dispels negative thoughts.

Brown aventurine, golden flecked with sparkling mica, improves energy, encourages creativity, and gives courage and serenity.

Dark bloodstone provides life vitality and shores up idealism. The masculine gem strengthens the will to do good. Bloodstone balances the chakras and increases one's talent. The stone is most helpful to overcome melancholy.

Calcite, in orange form, improves physical energy.

Chalcedony stimulates optimism and creativity.

Lithium is a mineral that banishes depression.

Magnetite eases anxiety, lifts low spirits, and soothes frustrations. The stone gives vigor to the astral body, opens the mind to new ideas, and promotes firmness of will. Magnetite bolsters physical energy by reinforcing the circulatory system and increasing oxygenation of blood. However, keep magnetite away from your computer or computer disks, since the slightly magnetic properties will cause loss of computer memory.

Jet dark marcasite is a physical strengthener and gentle energy giver. Marcasite is used widely as a stone in semiprecious jewelry. The gem aids in ability to cope with problems.

Peridot, a deep yellow-green stone, aids in development of inner vision, counteracts negative thoughts and opens the mind. The gem gives a tonic boost to the physical body. Qualities of the stone include soothing anger and cooling jealousy and other harmful emotional states.

Quartz crystals attract the power of light and energy. The long clear geometric crystals help to amplify and focus physical and mental energy.

Rose quartz, a delicate pink stone, stimulates imagination, heals bitterness, and gladdens the heart. The stone opens the physical and mental being to inner peace and beauty. Rose quartz helps to clear the channels to release bodily and mental energy.

Gray smoky quartz stimulates and purifies energy centers within the physical body. Smoky quartz grounds and stabilizes energies into useful channels. The stone will help you lift away sadness. This gem draws out negative energies and replaces them with positive, wholesome, and beneficial energy.

Ruby, the precious blood-red jewel, intensifies energy and gives courage.

Blue tourmaline carries a high electrical charge. Rub the stone briskly; the resultant spark can be directed wherever peaceful, positive energy is needed.

Blue and green turquoise shields from harmful influences, brings wisdom and rejuvenates and animates the physical body. If turquoise is used in combination with lithium, the stone and mineral work together to eradicate depression.

These beautiful stones are often sold with holes drilled in them so that you can sew the beads on the cloth where you wish. The gems can be placed in small pockets, if you prefer.

You can also gain the strength and endurance of the ancient forests by including bits of petrified wood to your talisman.

Are There Traditional Quilt Patterns for This Kind of Quilt? What Quilting Patterns Shall I Use to Finish the Quilt?

There are no traditional patterns for "energy," but the design of "Lone Star" or any of the star configurations would be beneficial to this type of work. The Ohio Star is a easy patchwork pattern. A Lone Star or Broken Star will challenge experienced quilters, but takes much longer than the usual one lunar month to construct.

If you choose not to use one of these star patterns, you can draw freehand stars, cut them out, and appliqué them randomly over the quilt top using hand-stitches or iron-on fusing web. This technique can also be used to apply images of the maker's hands, a powerful symbol.

Quilting patterns of radiating lines of stitching, representing energy emanating from the center of the quilt, should be used, as well as outlines of the maker's hands. Use simple outline motifs of the Sun, stars, flames, chili peppers, bamboo, or carnations. Add tracings of both your hands. Outlines of powerful natural phenomena such as lightning, storm clouds, or electric zig-zags are reminders of energy and power. Use red, yellow, or gold thread. Gold metallic thread is an attractive touch.

What Ideograms Shall I Use to Call on the Energy of Nature?

Calligraphic characters that express your wish for personal energy include: vigor, energy, spirit, courage, and tranquility. The ideogram for energy is *ch'i*. The brush strokes combine to form the thought "the universal breath or energy that gives us our material existence . . . ." Our energy of spirit is what forms our life. Tranquility, *an*, the world in order, is made up of "woman under man's roof" to show all is as it should be. Tranquility of heart is brought about by universal energies in harmony and balance.

Can You Suggest Some Fragrances That Will Enhance the Energy?

Fragrances of carnation, rosemary, and vanilla are revitalizing. Bathe using soap or oils scented with these essences. Burn a fragrant candle infused with one of these scents as you work. Stroke the essential oils of vanilla and carnation on the cloth after the completion of the work.

Tuck a vanilla bean and sprigs of the herbs rosemary and basil into hidden pockets or between the layers of fabric.

If you are tired or fatigued, lay the quilt in the sunshine. As the fire-force of the Sun warms the cloth, the scents of the herbs and flowers will rise and benefit you.

Summary

DAY TO BEGIN

Sunday: day of the spiritual, the Sun

Tuesday: day of Mars, power and energy

COLORS

crimson: happiness, strength, solar force

apple green: relieves depression, brightens outlook

green: healing, Druidic color of knowledge, wealth, insight

orange: intensification of emotions, bodily energy

flame red: strength of will, vitality

tan: a new beginning

purple-red: aids relief of depression

violet, purple: balances physical effect of warm oranges and yellow with cool spiritual and intellectual power

white: purity, balance of energies

yellow: self-confidence, personal power

yellow with indigo blue: increase psychic well-being

FABRIC MOTIFS

bamboo: resilient strength, natural grace, ability to flourish under adverse conditions

carnation: the Sun, power of fire, inner potential

chili peppers: heat, combustion

sun, stars, flames: released energy

trucks, dinosaurs, tigers: power, energy of nature

IDEOGRAMS

courage

energy

spirit

tranquility

vigor

STONES AND NATURAL AMULETS

agate: natural vitality, self-confidence, courage

amber: frees mental forces, calm

aventurine: courage, serenity, improves vitality

bloodstone: life vitality, will to do good

brass, gold, lava, jasper, chili peppers: associated with the energetic properties of heat and fire, change, release of energy

calcite: physical energy

chalcedony: creativity, optimism

crocidolite: overcome preoccupation with self

ebony, oak wood: strength and endurance

lithium: banish depression

magnetite: eases anxiety and depression, opens mind to new ideas, physical energy

marcasite: gentle energy, strength

peridot: inner vision, soothes anger and harmful emotional states

petrified wood: strength and endurance

quartz crystals: attracts power of light and energy, focuses energy

rose quartz: stimulates imagination, heals bitterness, clears channels to release bodily energy

ruby: courage, intensifies energy

smoky quartz: stabilizes energies into useful channels, draws out negative power

tourmaline: positive energy

turquoise: shields from harmful influences, wisdom, animates the physical body

HERBS AND FLOWERS

artemisa: feminine element of earth, physical endurance

black tea: courage, strength

carnation: energy, enhancement of positive vibrations

chili peppers: heat, energy of fire

masterwort: masculine fire element, physical stamina

olives: sacred to the Sun, peace

thistle: bodily vigor, protection against evil

thyme: good health, courage, psychic powers

vanilla: revitalization

FRAGRANCES

basil: energetic vibrations

carnation: multiplying energy

rosemary: energy, power of love

vanilla: revitalization, energy

STITCHING PATTERNS
outline of maker's hand: personal power

radiating lines: energy emission

stars: celestial power

*When you work you are a flute through whose
heart the whispering of the hours turns to music.*

—Kalil Gibran

Chapter 11

A Quilt for Healing

Mind and Body in Tune with Nature

Joy comes to those who have the heart to convert their pain to art.

—John D. Engle, Jr.

ealing was the traditional gift of wise women in ages past. The uses of herbs, stones, food, and the laying on of hands in order to induce a healthy body and mind in harmony with nature was sometimes looked upon with superstition. A gift that should have been received thankfully became regarded as a curse. In this age of science, the ability to achieve attunement to the rhythm of life in order to bring physical and mental wholeness is often regarded skeptically or is seen as something beyond the reach of simple remedies.

In order to work magic that affects another human, it is necessary to have their knowing permission. When a wish quilt is made to aid healing, either in spirit or body, it is proper to tell the ill person, "I am praying for you and making you something special." This is an affirmation of your belief that this person will become well.

Scott Cunningham calls visualization "the steering wheel of magic." Visualization is the most important part of any spell. You create an image in your mind, an image so real it can *become* real. Of course, you can't decide you can fly without an airplane or turn into a fish, no matter how hard you might want to—but you can picture a change you desire to occur in your life.

At all times as you cut and sew, see in your mind this friend or family member—or yourself—healthy and happy. Include in this work amulets for restoration of body and spirit, for they are indeed one. Often, the cure is a mental acceptance of a physical condition that cannot be changed.

The most famous example of the healing qualities of self-expression is the NAMES Project AIDS Memorial Quilt. Since 1987, The Quilt has grown from a neighborhood cause to an international symbol of love, hope, and inner healing. The Quilt does not wish for healing of the one who has passed on, that is of course impossible. Healing is desired instead for the partner and family left with a void once filled by an individual who was a loved—and loving—person. Though the panels are created out of the emotion of grief, there is hope sewn into each one that those who view the work will be moved to act, to remember those whom they love and to help increase the public awareness of the AIDS epidemic.

A group of quilters in Florida known as the South East Art Quilters (SEA Q) started a project to explore the process of working through the devastating experience of a natural disaster. After the hurricanes in the South Florida area during the early and mid-1990s, the eleven artists that comprise the group saw that the emotions of helplessness and frustration that the storms evoked had begun to affect their work.

A healing quilt incorporates nature's bounty to help get over a broken relationship.

They sought to bring to the community an insight into the curative ability of self-expression through their intimate media based on the quilting tradition. Beginning with a curated small local exhibit, they progressed to a three-year national touring exhibition. Their work can be seen in *Contemporary Pictorial Quilts, Fiberarts Design, International Quilting,* and numerous other respected publications.

An entire genre of quilts called "divorce quilts" has also been produced. These works demonstrate the reaction to a break in a relationship. The handwork expresses intense inner emotions that cannot be articulated to friends or other helpers. The quilts include clothing, pictures, phrases, broken wedding rings, even such things as mutilated representative body parts. The compositions are splashed with paint, run over by cars, slashed with knives. Some have been prominently displayed in store windows or presented to the "new"—or old—wife or husband.

What Is a Healing Quilt Used For?

A healing talisman quilt may be created for the renewal of physical or mental health. Construct a healing quilt incorporating the positive properties of nature's bounty to effect a self-cure from a broken relationship.

Sometimes a healing quilt will work out sadness; often the fabrication allows the maker to express the anger at his or her helplessness that cannot be verbalized. A quilt of this type is often ceremonially buried or burned after completion, to give a total sense of closure to a painful experience.

How Long Will It Take?

There is no set length of time that this composition should take, but keeping a regular schedule for working on it will strengthen your sense of purpose. Usually, I organize and construct a magic quilt over the course of about one lunar month.

When Is the Best Time to Start?

A kindness such as healing can be begun at any time that is convenient for you, but add ritual strength to your efforts by selecting the traditional day and hour. Healing comes under the auspices of Mercury, thus this project should be begun on a Wednesday. If your visualization sees this ailment as decreasing, begin on a waning Moon. If you prefer to visualize strength and energy increasing, or health flowing back into the afflicted one, utilize the waxing—growing—Moon. Sunrise is a time of renewal and rejuvenation. Noon gives physical strength and protection. Sunset is the time to cast away misery and pain and release harmful habits.

A special date to keep in mind for this type of quilt is February 26, marking the festival of Hygeia, the Roman goddess of health and well-being. The day celebrates physical vitality. If February 26 falls near the time you wish to begin your talisman, the day is an auspicious time and will aid to focus your intent in making the quilt.

How Shall I Prepare a Workbox?

The color of the box for this healing work may be selected from the list of healing colors given at the end of this chapter. But, in general, a blue or green sturdy cardboard container with a lid is suitable. Cleanse the box thoroughly with salt and sunshine for three days.

Healing energies may be increased in your creative materials by keeping the cloth and items in a cedar box or chest. If the hearty essence of red cedar has faded, lightly sand the inside surface of the wood to restore the fragrance or rub a bit of fresh aromatic cedar oil on the inner wooden surface. If you use cedar oil, wipe along the grain carefully with a clean cotton cloth to remove any excess, then fold new white tissue into the box so that the oil will not contact—and possibly stain—anything.

If you cannot use a cedar box, infuse a properly cleansed paper box with the fragrance of cedar by using small dabs of cedar oil; a layer of cedar chips under tissue paper; or chips of cedar wood, incense, or potpourri in a cloth bag.

How Big Shall I Make This Quilt?

The quilt could be large enough to wrap comfortingly around a distressed person, to sleep under, or simply hold for reassurance. The size is strictly up to you, the maker. A quilt for physical convalescence is often made in a size that can be wrapped around the ill person, draped over his or her lap or—minimally—large enough to cover the afflicted area.

A composition made for mental healing may be a size that can be displayed in such a way that the owner can draw strength from seeing it. The quilt could be framed or hung on a wall and measure 8½ inches by 11 inches or larger.

I have also seen works made in the shape of a stuffed animal—the herbs and charms concealed within, so that a child could carry the animal and sleep with it.

What Shall I Concentrate On While I Work?

Picture goodness, serenity, and the limitless vitality of nature being stitched into the quilt. Do not see the negative force of sickness but instead the positive aspects of good health. See wholeness of spirit and body in harmony with the world and those individuals in it.

Picture goodness, serenity, and the limitless vitality of nature stitched into the quilt.

What Materials Are Needed for This Project?

As you select your cloth, images and colors remember it is most important to keep your symbols consistent in meaning. This keeps the energy focused on the target of effect you desire to produce.

After you've made your decisions about cloth, inclusions, and embellishments, gather scissors, needles, pins, thimble, sewing thread, and cloth for your project. Don't forget a thin batting that can be of cotton, fleece, or washed cotton flannel. The batting can even be an old used blanket as long as no bad memories are tied to it.

Batting material is always the middle of the quilt sandwich: on top, the composition of fabrics, messages, materials and objects you select for power and positive mental associations; in the center, the batting to provide substance, stability and a cushion for the hidden items; at the underside of the quilt, a backing—a plain cloth to support the construction. Examine a handmade quilt or piece of quilted clothing to get the feel of the layer method if you are unfamiliar with the technique.

What Is My Beginning Dedication Ritual?

When planning your beginning dedication ritual, think of the entire process of selection of materials and construction of the quilt as a complete ritual even though it will encompass a number of days or weeks.

The art of healing is in the powers of the elements water and fire. A trip to the beach or a flowing river will bring you peace of mind to begin your task. Sit on the sand and watch the waves. Let your mind relax. Feel only the ancient rhythm of the sea, our mother. Bring back a shell, pinch of sand, or tiny piece of driftwood to include in your quilt.

If a trip to the shore is not possible, meditating by a small fire in the fireplace, a group of candles, or a fountain or other active water source can aid contemplation of the task before you.

Before a healing task, I often bathe using sandalwood soap. Sandalwood possesses high spiritual vibrations and is useful for healing work, protection, and the granting of wishes. Such ritual bathing is a time for bodily and mental cleansing. Use it as a time to relax to a state of introspection and dedication to your goal. Think through the purpose of your project and be honest about what you are trying to achieve.

As I bathe, I burn a purple, green, or blue candle—green and purple speed healing and draw extra power to your efforts while blue is the protective and remedial color. Before you light a candle, hold the taper between your palms as you think of the effect you are wishing for. Once again, this will help you define and strengthen your intent. Imagine yourself pushing your inner power into the candle so that the flame will release the energies into the atmosphere. Inscribe the candle with a word or symbol that represents the sickness— physical or mental—that you want to banish. Dress the candle with cedar, rose, or eucalyptus oil to aid healing powers. As the wax burns past the inscription of your desire, picture the problem being eaten by the flame and sent away from any influence on your mind or body.

At some time during the composition of the talisman, burn an incense of cedar or eucalyptus for purification and freedom from infirmity. If you have medications that you are taking, the bottles or containers should be placed near the burning candles or incense.

Incense of rose, sandalwood, or gardenia will bring an aura of peace and rehabilitation. Beautiful hand fans carved of sandalwood are available in most Oriental shops. As you waft the air with the opened fan, the gentle perfume is soothing to your mind.

What Fabrics Shall I Use?

In this instance, patches made of cloth from the clothes of the person intended to be restored to wholeness would be appropriate. Using the fabric-image transfer process, a snapshot or portrait of your subject may also be imprinted on cloth. The photo-to-fabric process—a technique to transfer photos to fabric using heat-sensitive paper with no damage resulting to the paper—may be done at home with a kit or by a copy shop. The photo used should be one taken when this person was healthy and happy. Also consider the textures of the cloth to be used. The texture may be soft and soothing or strong and defensive. The tactile character should communicate to you the quality you desire. Perhaps there is a certain type of cloth, such as satin or velvet, that has a particularly vivid force of memory attached—touching these fabrics can open a happy room from the past. Happiness is a strong medicine for curing sickness of the mind or body. Use it.

What Designs and Images Should Be Included?

Select your designs and colors thoughtfully with the qualities of inner peace, confidence, and healing in mind. New fabric with images of anemones, apples, cucumbers, lizards, red geraniums, nuts, snakes, onions, and peppermint may be used. Also consider clover, sacred to Mercury, the god of healing. Cloth with the print of clover is found abundantly in fabric stores before St. Patrick's Day.

Use fabrics like velvet or satin to provide sensual textures for healing.

Apples are so deeply associated with magic that it is impossible to list all the benefits of the fruit, called Fruit of the Gods, The Silver Bough, and the Tree of Love. The apple is used for love magic, as well as spells for immortality and bodily vigor. The famous sweet fruit is within the feminine element of water, sacred to Diana, Athena, and Venus, among others—including Zeus. Including the image of ripe apples and promising blossoms is to ask for powerful help.

American Indian totem or spirit animals can also be used to bring health. The bear represents strength and power and its mighty spirit is invoked for curing illness. So powerful is the bear that his pawprints are used as talismans to beseech good health. The humble turtle represents toughness and longevity. Birds have the ability to carry prayers upward to the spirits in the sky. Ants, the scurrying little insects, represent life's irritations. A small desert reptile, the strange horned toad aids with rheumatism and foot sores. Feverish babies and body sores will be soothed by the fearsome-looking gila monster.

In American Indian folklore, the mysterious snake bears petitions to the spirits in the underworld and guardians of springs and waters. The snake fetish may cure stomach and kidney ailments. A symbol of eternity, wisdom, psychic energy, health and virility, the snake is an ancient image in many cultures across the Earth.

Serpents are frequent motifs in Gypsy charms to ward against evil.

In European thought, the snake is also given an association with the healing power. A common motif which relates snakes with healing is the symbol of medicine—the caduceus, the sacred snake-twined staff of the physician. The image of the serpent is also a frequent motif in Gypsy charms to ward against evil. Snakes had entire temples dedicated to them in ancient Greece. Prosperous magicians and poor wise women carefully fed their sacred hearth-snakes with bowls of warm milk by the embers. In the oldest of European belief systems, a house snake was felt to be the representative of departed ancestors.

I have lived in many houses across the United States and in Japan, in the country and in town, and have always discovered a snake abiding under my front porch. My landlady in Japan advised, "One house, one snake. For health and luck."

Ornaments and jewelry depicting snakes are always popular, perhaps because of the beautiful sinuous form awakening a deep psychic resonance. Finding a serpent ornament made of the stones associated with curative energies, such as rose quartz or moonstone, would make a dramatic and effective addition to your magic healing quilt. Snake-print fabrics are always in vogue and add a striking note to a quilt, especially if used as a surrounding border.

Lizards living near or in the home are thought to be protective and help keep disease from the home. These lively reptiles are ruled by Mars. Currently, the image of lizards is easily found in textile prints and jewelry.

In Japanese folklore, the leaves of the iris convey healing power and freedom from disease when steeped in a springtime bath. Chrysanthemum petals in water give longevity. Tortoise shells (or small octagons representing them) are another charm for health and longevity as the lowly turtle is thought to live 10,000 years. A configuration of six gourds is a motif for good health.

Fruit and vegetable motifs are readily found in kitchen textile sections, on towels or curtains as well as bolt-yardage fabrics. Textiles with images of practically any animal or plant can be found in a shop that handles quilter's supplies. Unusual designs of unexpected subjects—from lizards to wizards—can be found in the children's fabric section of a cloth or craft store.

If you cannot find a design or motif you feel you need, consider stenciling or painting the image on plain cloth. I have several simple stencil books from the children's craft section that are very helpful to me. One booklet has outlines of sea creatures and cost less than $2.00; the same series has booklets of African animals, earth-moving machines, boats, bugs, and flowers. A favorite stencil collection of mine has desert images in the popular Southwestern style with designs for snakes, turtles, bears, and howling coyotes, as well as stylized lightning, clouds, cactus, and mountains. Craft stores have a wide variety of stencils, stamps, and fabric paint that are easy to use and yield very satisfactory results. Even crayons may be used with pleasing results.

Fabric should be herbally bathed and charged, using the water steeped with herbs, plants, and stones listed that are associated with curative energies.

Selected herbs, plant parts, stones, shells, or other items should be set aside for inclusion within the work. Remember to include these objects behind the top patches so that they will be hidden securely within the composition of the quilt. Pockets may be sewn on the front or back face of the cover to be used to hold notes, prayers, or other changeable parts you wish to include.

Dried plants, flowers, and herbs are usually too brittle to sew to the outer surface of the quilt, so I recommend including them between the layers of cloth. Stones and shells may be fastened to the surface with ties or have a small hole bored so that they may be sewn on.

What Plants Can Aid My Goal of Healing?

Healing plants, herbs, and wood can be included between the layers of fabric, hidden in small pockets, or placed in small bags and sewn or tied onto the surface of the quilt.

Beads, buttons, or twigs of the rowan (*Sorbus aucuparis*), also known as Mountain Ash, can be attached to the quilt. Rowan is a powerful plant. It represents the masculine gender and is sacred to the god Thor. Rowan conveys the virtues of restoration of health, protection, success, and psychic power. Aside from including rowan in your magic healing quilt, carry the berries or bark to aid in recuperation. If the quilt is to be hung like a wall banner, consider using a small rowan branch to support the cloth.

General healing herbs to include in your quilt are bay, cinnamon, eucalyptus, peppermint, sage, and sassafras. For sickness involving loss of sleep, use elderberry, lavender, lemon balm, sandalwood, and vanilla. To ease stress, try lavender, pennyroyal, and cumin.

The spicy carnation (*Dianthus carophyllus*) is a masculine flower with the protection of the Sun and the deity Jupiter. The flowers and scent give strength, rejuvenation, and protection. Cinnamon (*Cinnamomum zeylanicum*) raises intense spiritual vibrations for aid in recuperation and the stimulation of protective forces.

The Mexican aloe (*Sabila sagrada*, agave) is used in magic spells to invoke the "sacred initiate," a sleeping goddess. The plant is considered the home to a goddess who can be put into a favorable mood through offerings and prayers. If she is pleased, her gifts to bestow are health, wealth, and peace.

Indeed, there are so many herbal remedies for every ill, general and specific, that it is difficult to list them all. A visit to a holistic shop or health food store can provide you with suggestions for what to include in cases of specific illnesses. Remember to observe extra precautions if you are pregnant.

Scott Cunningham's *Encyclopedia of Magical Herbs* has a complete treatment of this subject. The following list of suggestions has been cross-referenced using Cunningham's work, *The Herb Bible*, by Peter McHoy and Pamela Westland (Barnes & Noble, 1994), and the *Illustrated Encyclopedia of Herbs*, Claire Kowalchik and William Hylton, editors (Rodale Press, 1987).

Please remember this information is intended as a reference, not as a medical manual or a guide to self-treatment. I caution you not to embark upon self-treatment of physical or mental illness without competent professional assistance. The information in this book is not intended to substitute for any treatment that may have been prescribed by your physician.

Include leaves, twigs, flowers, or seeds. If the desired plant is not available, an image of the herb can be used, but naturally this is not as effective.

angelica: healing incense, aid for digestive disorders

apples: healing, good health, love, magic

basil: nervous headaches, digestive upsets, soothes tempers between two people, increases feelings of sympathy

bay, cinnamon, eucalyptus, peppermint, sage, sassafras: general healing

burdock: (leaves) relief from gout

camphor: flu and colds, respiratory ailments, promotes chastity

carnation: sacred to god Jupiter and the Sun; strength, rejuvenation, protection

cedar: takes away bad dreams, eases head colds, gives protective energy

cinnamon: stimulation of protective forces, energy

cypress: to be used at times of crisis, eases mind of grief, general healing

elder: sacred to many Mother Goddess figures; aids in fever, toothaches, rheumatism, warts, difficulty in sleeping; extremely protective

elderberry, lavender, lemon balm, vanilla: restful sleep

fennel: digestion, liver and kidney problems

flax: dizziness, lumbago, general healing

garlic: guards against the plague, absorbs diseases, protection from evil

groundse: good dental health

knotweed: strengthens the eyes

lavender, pennyroyal, cumin: easing of stress

lettuce: gives peaceful sleep, guards against seasickness

linden: brings sleep when used with lavender

marjoram: soothes depression, brings happiness

mint: general good health, relief of headaches and stomach problems

myrrh: offered as incense to Ra and Isis; healing, aid to meditation

nutmeg: wards off rheumatism, cold sores, sties, boils, aids teething in infants

oak: long life, protection against illness and pain

onions: ability to absorb illness; healing, guard against infections and sickness, take away warts

pine: increase fertility, aid to the ill, ward away sickness, promote vigor in old age

purslane: peaceful sleep

rose: general good health, banish headaches, calm personal stress

rosemary: good health, youthfulness, healing, peaceful sleep, dispel depression

rowan: sacred to god Thor; restoration of health, protection, success

rue: recuperation and healing

sandalwood: brings spiritual awareness; healing, freeing magic wishes and power

sorrel: (leaves) preserves the heart against disease, recuperation from illness and wounds

tansy: health and longevity; protection against fever

thistle: healing, virility, drives away melancholy

thyme: good health

What Colors Will Carry a Beneficial Effect?

Greens and blues are most widely used as medicinal tints— these are the colors used for contemporary doctor's and nurse's uniforms. Green is associated with the heart chakra— love, healing, and empathy are related in green, as are inspiration and intuition. Emerald green represents tranquility, hope, freshness—the natural vitality of healthy earth energy.

Green is cooling for such ailments that contain infection. Headaches caused by tension and disharmony need the soothing power of leaf shades.

As you work with greens and blues, think of the sparkle of leaves and water in the sunlight, the beauty of a green bud unfolding into a flower, or a serene garden or pond. In visualizing an aura of nature's green and blue, caring, healing, and harmony will be projected.

Color is an important part of Chinese folk and medicinal cures. Color is used to strengthen the beneficial life force ch'i and diminish the evil effects of imbalance and disharmony in the flow of life and character that make up one's personality. One example of using color in a meditational capacity is the Green Tara Meditation. Tara is a sacred enlightened person, known for her compassion. Her Chinese name is Lu Du Fwo Mu, the Green-colored Mother of the Buddha. As Sakyamuni traveled on his way toward Enlightenment, he faced many trials and temptations. Green Mother Tara protected him. Green Mother Tara wears flowing iridescent green robes and a distinctive dharma cap with five points. She is known for curing sickness, especially cancer, and protecting the supplicant from unexpected harm.

Indigo, enhanced with warm orange, focuses thoughts on correcting lung problems.

By gentle meditation on her colors of flowing green, physical and mental health problems may be eased. With regular practice, patience, wisdom, and compassion are said to be increased. A complete Green Tara Meditation is explained in detail in *Living Color*, by Sarah Rossback and Lin Yun (Kodansha, 1994).

Blue-green, mint, and aqua are aligned with the colors of spring. They are auspicious colors associated with lively youthful qualities. Light blue is a curative shade, related to the throat chakra, center of communication. Blue hues are useful in medical problems with the throat area, muscular spasms, and menstrual cramps or other discomfort associated particularly with what were once called "female problems."

Sky blue is helpful for spiritual illnesses brought on by problems communicating with others or blockage in artistic, creative affairs. Indigo is used in healing ailments involving the eyes, ears, and nose, as well as mental and nervous problems. Indigo has the ability to strengthen the astral nature of its wearer. Use this hue enhanced with warm orange to focus your thoughts for correction of lung problems.

Although real indigo is expensive, an indigo-dyed natural fabric commonly available is blue denim, such as blue-jean fabric. Denim from jeans worn by the person for whom the assistance is intended would increase the power of a healing or protective quilt both by combining color and personalization of vibrations. If possible, cut the garment so that an intact pocket can be used within the quilt. Write your wish concisely and clearly on a plain white piece of paper and place it in the pocket.

Soft, worn old indigo cotton cloth is treasured in Japan to use as diapers for sickly babies or as underwear for elderly people who are weakened by disease. The indigo is said to have curative and disinfective properties, and using old cloth is felt to bring to fruition a wish for long life.

The warming color of red will give its intensity to problems involving the circulation or blood. Red, orange, and yellow used together give warmth and energy to one debilitated by chronic ailments, age, or extreme melancholy. Touches of the energy of orange help with problems of the abdomen and lungs. Those suffering from high blood pressure and heart problems should avoid red, however, and use light green, light blue, white, or black.

Red, purple, and pink are said to help problems stemming from immunological problems. The combination of bright blue, red, and green is an antidote for despair as these are the colors of hope and life.

Purple is used for relief of ailments of brain function and those created by mental stress. Tension, sleeplessness, and disorders aggravated by unresolved mental conflicts can be eased by the use of purple. Reddish purple aids in combating chronic depression. Headaches are eased with green and pinks.

White is a combination of colors, a blend yielding peace, love, and protection. When visualizing protection and healing around a subject, white carries the soul to meet and soothe the troubled spirit. Picture an aura of white within and around yourself, then push the radiance outward gently to envelop the afflicted or troubled subject. Distance is no barrier to this projection. If visualization of this kind is difficult for you, start by imagining a wide, glowing white ribbon swirling around your body and away to the one you wish to help.

White will aid in clearing and unifying your intentions. Clearing your thoughts with the mental picture of the purity of white will help in gaining rapport with your work before proceeding with the appropriate color choice. Within the handiwork of a healing quilt, white is a useful color for setting off individual colors, giving them a defined border, and amplifying and intensifying the effect.

There is a wide array of color association with specific healing practices. *The Women's Spirituality Book* by Diane Stein (Llewellyn, 1987) is a useful reference for more complete details.

Where Shall I Place a Secret Wish?

A magic healing quilt, and any of the other magic wish quilts, should have pockets provided to place written wishes or pictures that show your intent.

Pockets can be made by cutting a small rectangle of cloth (approximately 4 inches by 6 inches). Turn under ½ inch all around the rectangle of fabric and press the cloth so that the fold stays back. Pin the pocket where you want it on the quilt top. Stitch evenly around three sides of the rectangle—refer to a shirt pocket for an idea of this type of construction. Items may be placed in the pocket, then the top stitched closed.

Sew the pockets from your own or your friend's jeans or shirts to the quilt patches on the front or back of the cover. A pocket can be removed from a garment by carefully picking out the stitching. The complete pocket can then be sewn where you wish to put a little hiding place on the quilt.

Another method is to cut a patch or strip from a garment and leave the useable pocket (such as a hip or shirt pocket) in place. Sew this strip directly into the quilt top. Pockets provide places to tuck in written wishes and intents, as well as concealing additional herbal charms, photos, or meaningful symbols of your faith. For instance, when visualizing vibrant health, small pictures cut from sports magazines showing a favorite activity may be hidden within the pockets.

Write the exact wish you have in mind.

"I wish for the pain in my arms to disappear."

"I want my son to recover from the sadness of losing his wife."

"I want my mother's headaches to be eased."

State it simply and clearly. Fold the paper while strongly picturing the completion of the wish. Press it between your palms, then place it inside a pocket. Sew or button the pocket closed.

If you are doing the sewing by hand, denim can be difficult to stitch through due to the thickness, but putting on a pocket does not require much stitching. Simplest of all would be using a hot glue gun, but this removes certain aspects of personal dedication to the task. The size of the stitches is not important, only the loving intent of the hands that make them.

Beautiful small portraits of Christian saints are available at religious supply stores and are generally inexpensive. These once-living individuals have been associated with miraculous healing powers, often gaining their sainthood for this quality of spirituality. There are patron saints for every type of sickness and affliction. Pictures or small charms of saints may be stitched to the fabric surface or placed in pockets.

PARTIAL LIST OF CHRISTIAN SAINTS THAT MAY BE INVOKED IN CASES OF SPECIAL NEED

arthritis: Saint James

blindness: Saint Odilla

bodily ills: Our Lady of Lourdes

bruises: Saint Amalberga

cancer, skin disease: Saint Peregrine

colic, stomach problems, ulcers: Saint Charles Borromeo

convulsions: Saint Scholastica

cramps: Saint Maurice

cures: Saint Benedict

deafness: Saint Francis de Sales

desperate situations: Saint Rita, Saint Jude

epilepsy: Saint Genesius

fever, foot trouble: Saint Peter

gallstones: Saint Liberius

headaches: Saint Denis

healing of wounds, loneliness, tumors: Saint Rita

insanity, mental illness, nerves: Saint Dymphna

invalids: Saint Roque

rheumatism: Saint James the Greater

spiritual help: Saint Vincent de Paul

sudden death: Saint Barbara

toothache: Sant Apollonia

Angels, gods, goddesses, and unusual mortals with special powers are invoked and petitioned for help in cases of health problems. You may feel moved to include one or more of these mighty individuals in expressing your desire for wholeness.

ANGELS

Och: angel of the Sun, dominion over sickness, confers ability to heal the sick

Phul: the angel of the Moon, talent to destroy evil spirits on and in water, ability to cure dropsy (the abnormal retention of water within the body)

Saint Raphael: the Archangel; Regent of the Sun, angel of science and knowledge; angel of healing

GODS, GODDESSES, AND UNUSUAL MORTALS

Deities from many cultures are included on this list so that you may select one that appeals to your own ethnic or philosophical background.

Abowie: (Ghanaian) goddess of healing; aids in problems of sterility

Addus: (Celtic) god with healing powers

Aesculapius: (a Greek mortal later elevated to deity) a mortal who was given the sacred gift of healing, able to give aid and ease in all manner of maladies and delivery from torment

Angitia: (Italian) goddess of healing through skillful use of medicinal plants and charms

Anquit: (Egyptian) goddess of life and health

Bast: (Egyptian) beautiful cat goddess of healing and happiness, warmth of the sun

Bakira: (Japanese) god who protects the skin from evil spirits carrying diseases

Carna: (Roman) goddess of health; aids problems with digestion, vital organs and the heart

The Camenae: (early Roman) practical goddesses who cure disease and care for springs and wells

Chiron: (Greek mortal centaur) a centaur, half man and half horse, wise and kindly, who taught the healing arts to mortals

Eshmun: (Phoenician) God of healing

Fand: (Celtic) Goddess of kind healing; her emblem is the bird

Gwelebhot: (Penebscot Indian) God who gave man medicinal herbs

Honani: (Hopi Indian) the supernatural badger-god who taught men about medicinal herbs and plants for healing cures

Hygea (Greek) or **Hygeia** (Roman): Goddess of health; She is the preventer, the patroness of foresight to avoid illness

Ibeyi: (West Indian, African) sacred infant twins, preventers and healers of childhood illness

Inle: (West Indian, African) healer of all illnesses, representative of androgynous nature, patron of homosexuals

Kamaka: (Hawaiian) god of healing

Obatala: (West Indian, African) god who protects from head injuries, mental illness, blindness, and paralysis; dispels evil

Oya: (West Indian, African) goddess, guardian of death, who opens the portals to the afterlife; protects from accidents involving electricity and illnesses concerning the respiratory tract

Sekhmet: (Egyptian) the lion goddess; fierce mistress of healing who drives away sickness

Uni: (Finnish) God of sleep

What Stones, Amulets, and Extras May Be Added for Regaining Health?

Abalone is the shell of the clam, Haliotis. The sea green and blue colors strengthen muscular tissue, especially those near the heart.

Agate reduces fever, hardens tender gums.

Amber protects against disease and infections, draws out pain and unhappiness, and shields the digestive system.

Amethyst is the "sobriety stone," aiding in recovery from alcohol addiction and easing anxiety.

Aquamarine is a blue-green beryl stone, useful in dealing with problems of the glands, eyes, and stomach. Relieves toothache.

Buckeye, the horse chestnut, protects and relieves rheumatism and hemorrhoids.

Buzzard feather relieves rheumatism and arthritis.

Brown feather encourages good health.

Green calcite is beneficial for kidneys, spleen and pancreas.

Cedar wood heals and protects.

Citrine of the yellow quartz variety aids restoration of good circulation and strengthens the immune system. Helps with diabetes and depression.

Coral promotes general physical well-being. Aids in anemia, bladder conditions, and whooping cough. Said to be an aid in digestive disorders and epilepsy in children.

Copper wards against arthritis and rheumatism.

Eucalyptus aids healing and convalescence.

Garnet protects against dullness of spirit, helps with any blood problems. General good tonic for the entire physical and mental systems.

Red jasper claimed to be useful in remediation of blood disorders, digestion problems, and bladder trouble.

Jet prevents deep depression; eases migraine and eye pain.

Magnetite tones for the endocrine system.

Malachite, a rich green copper carbonate, the stone of Queen Guinevere. Used in treatment of asthma, toothache, and rheumatism.

Marcasite is a gentle overall physical strengthener.

Oak wood heals and protects.

Olive shells promote general healing.

Pearl fights infection, promotes robust immune system.

Peridot banishes insomnia, aids digestion, physical tonic.

Quartz in its clear form amplifies all beneficial qualities of curative energy and intent.

Rock crystal eases pain located anywhere in the physical body. Aids in alleviating dizziness, kidney problems, and diarrhea.

Selenite calms and clears troubled minds, stabilizes emotions. In his handbook *The Mystical Crystal* (C. W. Daniel Co. G.B., 1993), Geoffrey Keyte cautions that this stone is very powerful in medicinal energies and should be used with caution.

Tiger's eye is useful in a healing quilt as it counteracts tendencies toward hypochondria and psychosomatic illness.

Turquoise aids in mitigating heart problems, including those of lost love and loneliness. Turquoise is a general healing stone if there is nothing specific to be found.

Tourmaline guards against lymphatic disease and anemia.

Yellow topaz soothes nerves, aids in achieving healthful, deep sleep. Improves sense of taste, blood circulation, and aids repair of liver ailments. Guards against tension and releases gloomy thoughts.

Walnut wood is good for healing and strength.

Zircon is a general rejuvenator that eases childbirth, insomnia, and liver dysfunction.

From the partial list above, it can be seen that gems and minerals are given a plethora of healing qualities. It can be beneficial to your purpose to prepare a gem elixir and wash or sprinkle any of the materials used for your quilt talisman in this liquid. Gem elixirs are particularly helpful for improvement of problems arising from the darker emotions, such as jealousy or fear, either directed toward the subject or harbored within.

Prepare a gem elixir by placing the selected stone or combination of stones in a clear new glass or crystal bowl—crystal will intensify the powers of the stones. Add pure water; rainwater gathered in a thunderstorm is ideal. Place the bowl of water and stones in the full sunlight from dawn to dusk. It may be necessary to move the bowl in order to follow the path of the sunlight. After sunset, pour off the water into a clean new blue, amber, or green bottle. Cork or cap the bottle tightly until use.

Gem elixir kept in an amber or golden bottle is said to be efficacious for problems involving the nerves, kidneys, liver, and excretory organs. A green bottle will increase the effect of the elixir on the sympathetic nervous system and is considered useful for promoting general healing and restoration and balance of the systems. If you are not sure what color to use, use green. A cobalt blue flask will have a cooling effect for pain and infection. The blue hue will relax, subdue bad influences, soothe nervousness, and increase an antiseptic quality. (*The Ancient Art of Color Therapy*, Linda Clark, Devin-Adair, CT, 1975.)

It is said that this elixir may be taken internally at the rate of ten drops, twice a day for one month. Gem elixirs may be used in conjunction with other forms of treatment without interfering with that treatment. I feel it is more effective to use the resulting potion as an addition to your daily bath or to sprinkle the items to be used in your healing quilt, or immerse the cloth. Allow any fabric treated in this manner to dry thoroughly, then iron it well before use.

Are There Traditional Quilt Patterns for This Kind of Quilt?

Any traditional quilt pattern with a depiction of stars can be used. There are many, in various degrees of difficulty. There are also several patterns with geometric leaves that would be beautiful done in robust greens.

What Ideograms Shall I Use?

Ideograms representing wisdom, energy, love, patience, courage, vigor, and devotion are suggested for use. The character for wisdom is a complex one in thought, although not in artistic formation—the pictograms for spoken, mouth, oath, and Sun put together the thought that knowledge, like the rays of the Sun, brings goodness to the world. To be made whole, in heart or body, all the virtues of wisdom, love, courage, and patience are called upon.

What Quilting Shall I Use to Finish the Piece?

For a stitching design, use a combination of tracings of your hands and the sick person's hands, hearts linked at the point, magic (five-pointed) stars, and twining flowers and vines (harmony of nature). An outline of the powerful bear or mystic healing snake may be used. Stitch with red or white thread.

Chih *is the Chinese ideogram for wisdom.*

I Want to Add a Beneficial Scent. What Should It Be?

Stroke the finished quilt with allspice and sew the ground spice between the fabric layers. The scent is vitalizing and excellent for convalescents. Sandalwood and eucalyptus oils are curative and effective in speeding recuperation after a long illness.

A practical caution: Magic is not to be used in place of professional medical or psychiatric attention, but only to augment it.

Summary

DAY TO BEGIN
Wednesday: day of Mercury

COLORS
blue-green, mint, aqua: lively youthfulness

blue, light: the throat chakra, communication

blue, red, and green: used together, these colors lift despair and depression

blue, sky: spiritual illness, creative affairs

greens and blues: healing properties

green: the heart chakra, love, empathy, inspiration

green, emerald: earth energy, tranquility, hope

green and pink (together): headache

indigo: eyes, ears, nose, nervous problems

orange: abdomen and lungs

purple: the brain, mental stress

red: circulation of blood

red, orange, and yellow: energy to one debilitated from chronic illness

red, purple, and pink: immunological problems

red-purple: chronic depression

white: peace, love, protection, cleanliness, healing, energy boost

FABRIC MOTIFS

apples: health, magic, divine help

bears: healing power

clover: sacred to god, Mercury

fruits and vegetables, in particular cucumbers, onions, peppermint, garlic: health and bounty of Earth

lizards: protection, health

photographs: of person to receive healing

snakes: eternity, wisdom, health, virility

IDEOGRAMS

courage

devotion

energy

love

patience

vigor

wisdom

HERBS, STONES, AND NATURAL AMULETS

The list of herbs, stones and natural amulets is so lengthy
that I will not repeat it here. Please refer to the sections in
this chapter on page 167 and 175.

FRAGRANCES

allspice: vitality, convalescence

eucalyptus: speeds recuperation

sandalwood: curative vibrations

STITCHING PATTERNS

bear, bear tracks: healing

five-pointed stars: magic to speed healing

hearts linked at the point: love, power through
friendship and love

leaves: nature's energy, good health

snake: healing, magic, energy of nature

twining vines and flowers: strength and vitality of
nature

your hand: the healing touch, personal wishes

Chapter 12

A Healing Example

A Gift of Health and Peace

Rings and other jewels are not gifts, but
apologies for gifts. The only gift is a portion
of thyself.

—Ralph Waldo Emerson

"*I* want my mother's headaches to be eased." When I
wrote this down, I realized I meant more than her
physical pain. Her headaches were caused by the stress of
caring for a demanding and critical parent. For her, healing
had to be both physical and mental. My mother needed help.

The day to begin was Wednesday, the day ruled by the
god Mercury. I drove to the beach and walked at the edge of
the surf, clearing my mind for the creative power to enter.
The art of healing is contained within the elements of water
and fire. The eternal rhythm of the sea soon relaxed the
mind-chatter within that obscures much of our artistic and
spiritual side. I began to plan the piece I wanted to make for
my mother.

I debated as to the time of the lunar cycle to begin the talisman. If the Moon was on the increase, growth of her energy
and health could be projected. With the Moon on the wane,
there could be a lessening of pain, a decrease of stress, and an

183

unbinding of her feelings of guilt. The Moon on the decrease seemed to be the optimal choice, working on the cause of the headaches, rather than the headaches themselves.

When I returned home, I called my mother to get her consent for my endeavor. After I hung up, I consecrated and lit three candles: blue (healing), purple (to aid in spiritual endeavors and problems dealing with mental stress), and white (for additional spiritual power and concentration of healing energy). I prepared a small red cedar box that had been Mother's to hold the quilt materials. The chest was given a thorough cleansing with salt, wiped with fresh cedar oil, aired, and lined with new white tissue.

I decided to make the quilt about 45 inches square. Mother could fold the gift at the foot of her bed during the day or throw it over her knees in the evening.

The next day, I selected a snapshot we had taken when I was much younger. Mother was smiling, in good health and relaxed. It was the way I remembered her and the way I wanted her to be again, for her own sake.

I took this little snapshot and had the picture transferred to a square of vibrant yellow cotton cloth. Before the transfer process, I charged the fabric in pure water with carnation oil to give the power of rejuvenation. The yellow would draw physical energy, and put power within the talisman of the quilt. The fabric was selected and prepared, pressed, folded and stored in the cleansed cedar box. When not in use, I kept the box tucked under my bed.

The yellow square was sewn to the center of the "sandwich" of batting and backing. The sunshine color formed an energy-drawing heart for the composition. Before I sewed the square down, I prepared a handwritten statement of my intentions in making this quilt.

I wrote "I want my mother's headaches to be eased. I want happiness to return to my mother's life. I desire mental and physical energy for my mother." This note was folded inside a Valentine card she had sent me several years ago. The card and note were placed behind the central yellow photo square.

After I pinned the yellow square down, I began to add strips of fabric around the edges of the square. Emerald green would bring love and aid her in maintaining empathy. The rich green would aid in holding the stabilizing energy of earth, and give a sense of tranquility and hope. The green cloth was charged overnight in pure water, simmered with pinches of cinnamon, peppermint, and sage—all herbs for general healing.

The green strips were sewn into place on one side. Under each patch I put a teaspoon of whole cumin seeds for easing stress. Then each open side of the green strips was pinned down firmly to hold the cumin in place and prepare them for the next patches. A 3-inch strip of white cotton (peace, love, protection, and energy) that had been charged in pure water and carnation petals for protection and rejuvenation was sewn all the way around the green. Carnations are my mother's favorite flower, so an extra layer of meaning was present. The white section was folded down into place and pinned.

Next I included four strips, each about 5 inches wide and each of a different fabric design carrying images that would add power to my request. I selected a bright print of vegetables and fruits, to symbolize the bounty and vitality of earth. They would also remind me of my mother's love of good food and cooking. Orange, yellow, and red—colors to give life back to one debilitated by chronic pain and depression— sparkled with energy over this print. Vigorous green leaves twined around the vegetables, flashing the green of nature's healing color—headaches caused by tension and disharmony need the soothing of leaf shades.

The second fabric was deep blue with small bright golden stars scattered over it. This would represent the curative powers of blue and the celestial magic of the stars.

The third fabric was a print of round, red apples, the fruit of Venus that brings health and love.

The final strip was from a white shirt from my father. My father was the image of protection and love to my mother. I cut the shirt down the front so that the pocket was included.

Dark colors were charged together with pure water and the herbs lavender, peppermint, and cinnamon (energy, healing, and easing of stress). The white cloth was charged with cinnamon (protection and energy).

Charge cloth in cinnamon, peppermint, and sage . . . all are herbs for general healing.

勇
気

*Ying is the ideogram
for courage.*

When all these were suitably sewn down, three small round shards of turquoise were placed under the blue section. Turquoise vibrates with general healing qualities and aids in dispelling feelings of loneliness and depression.

Using indigo (protection and general healing) dyed cloth from a pair of my denim blue jeans, I surrounded the entire composition out to the edges of the quilt. I cut so that the hip pocket was included in one side. This provided a wide, plain blue section to serve as a field for calligraphy, stitching patterns, and embellishments.

Ideograms for patience, courage, and energy were selected. I appliquéd the Chinese characters using black cloth and iron-on fabric bonding film. One character was bonded at each of three corners.

At the final corner I drew around my right (power) hand with a sliver of sandalwood (adds an aura of peace and rehabilitation) soap to mark it on the denim. Using the splinter of soap I drew a simple design of leaves and five-pointed stars all the way around the edges of the quilt. Soap will not brush off as chalk will or leave a permanent mark or stain like ink or pencil. Soap makes the passage of the needle through the cloth easier. Lines were drawn over the calligraphy characters, but not intersecting the tracing of my hand or over the denim pocket.

Over the next several days, I stitched through the soap lines and all three layers of cloth, batting, and backing. This is the basic traditional quilting process. Because I wanted the stitches to show, I used the sashiko method which is simply a medium sized (about ⅛ inch long) even running stitch. A running stitch is the in-and-out plain sewing stitch you may have used to repair something. Thicker thread, such as pearl cotton, embroidery cotton, or silk is better to use than sewing thread as it shows up better, but a double strand of sewing or quilting thread may be used.

As I worked, I pictured as vividly as possible my mother as she had been, happy, singing. I purposefully pushed as much as I could of the pictured happiness and love into every stitch. Some evenings as I worked I would think of the Green Mother Tara meditation.

When the pattern stitching was finished, I prepared a strip of black cloth that would be used for binding the edges of the quilt. I needed four 45-inch sides, plus 6 inches "just in case." The black fabric was charged with cinnamon and carnation, dried in the moonlight, and ironed the next day. Then I cut the fabric in a 2½-inch-wide bias strip to use as the binding. If the bias cutting is a problem, wide cotton quilt binding can be purchased and charged—a much simpler process.

Every evening as I worked, I burned blue and purple candles or an incense of rose, gardenia, or sandalwood to help focus my mental energy on my intentions of peace and healing.

After the entire construction was quilted (pattern stitched over all) and bound with black binding tape around the edges so that no raw edges were showing, I laid the almost finished talisman in its box and put it under the bed to dream over. Two days later I felt that I knew what other items should be used for embellishments.

I added buttons made of oak and cedar from trees growing near our old house. To do this for your quilt, use a twig as big as your finger. Cut the twig carefully across the width of the wood using a fine hacksaw or sharp knife. Watch your fingers! Drill or burn two small holes in the middle of the disc of wood. Sew the buttons on firmly.

Using a jet necklace from my grandmother, I unstrung seven beads and attached them randomly around the emerald green fabric—jet dispells depression and lifts spirits. I also used turquoise (good health) totem fetish beads in the forms of a bear, fish, and a turtle (health, perseverance, and longevity), which I had bought at a craft store. Five beads of tiger's eye (avoiding a tendency for hypochondria) were sewn on the surface of the white fabric near the wish pocket.

At the same craft store, I purchased a yard each of narrow satin ribbon in the healing shades of blue and green. These ribbons were laid together then knotted in the center, leaving streamers of the length. I stitched these to the left side of the quilt.

The two pockets remained to be filled. At a local religious store I selected three small saints cards. One is of Saint Denis, a saint who is concerned with headaches. The second card is of Saint Rita, one who has influences over loneliness, healing of inner wounds, and situations often felt to be without hope. These colorful pictures were placed in the white shirt pocket and the shirt button fastened. The final card, placed in the denim pocket, was of Mother Mary, a maternal figure I feel represents the Eternal Mother Goddess. Mother Mary and a dried red rose were slipped in the denim pocket and the top of the fabric sewn closed. Once more I folded the quilt and laid it in its cedar chest. After two nights of sleep I felt that nothing more was to be added to the composition. I wrapped the work in new white tissue and nestled it in the wooden box. I gave it to my mother as a birthday gift the following month.

Chapter 13

The AIDS Quilt

Healing Personal Inner Wounds

Someone, I tell you, will remember us.

—Sappho

*T*he power of inner healing is given to those who seek it by mindfully working and thinking of their loss rather than hiding it and, like a hidden splinter, letting it scab, callous, or fester. The most famous example of the power of inner healing that a talismanic creation can produce is the AIDS/NAMES Memorial Quilt.

The AIDS/NAMES Memorial Quilt is a tribute of love, as well as a memorial to a horrific episode in our history. Its beauty is a splendor wrought of sadness. It is as a stone marked with time and history—not just of a single person, but a changing, challenging era. Like The United States Holocaust Memorial Museum or The Vietnam War Memorial, the quilt is a memorial we must see and wish we had never had to see.

Recognition should be given to Cleve Jones of San Francisco, California, the originator of this incredibly powerful eulogy. Jones was distressed and deeply concerned by the deaths caused by AIDS (Acquired Immune. More than 1,000 San Franciscans died in the period between 1980 and 1987. Searching for a way to express the grief he and his friends were experiencing, he gathered a small group "to take all of our individual experiences and stitch them together to make something that had strength and beauty." In a meeting in an empty storefront on Market Street, the idea of the AIDS Memorial Quilt was born.

The mission of the NAMES Project is to demonstrate the enormity of the AIDS epidemic by showing the humanity behind the statistics. Each panel depicts an individual, a person rather than a statistic, represented through symbols and representative items from their life . . . an individual lost but to our memories. As you view the quilt stretching across a field or hanging on a wall, the enormity of our losses is indelibly illustrated.

Reconciliation of personal grief is not a selfish goal.

By participating in the quilt, a creative form of expression and inner healing is offered. Reconciliation of personal grief is not a selfish goal. Such an experience is painful, but can be the last and best gift that one who has left can give. It should inspire spiritual growth and beneficial introspection of your own life.

Hopefully, the memorial quilt will inspire people to become involved in a community response to the AIDS epidemic. Unfortunately, the episode is continuing, an ongoing waking nightmare. AIDS is the leading cause of death of Americans between the ages of 25 and 44.

The loss of a companion leaves a void in our life that seems overwhelming. In the act of creating this visible admission of pain and love, a personal grief can be changed from an inner sorrow to closure, acceptance, and hope for the future. Add components to the panel that will assuage your feelings of loss, as well as establish your psychic connection with the intent of the quilt.

Begin a project for inner healing, such as a panel for the AIDS quilt, on a Wednesday, the day sacred to the god Mercury. Mercury serves as a messenger to the Gods and carries the caduceus, the sacred staff of the healer. The emblems of green clover and the serpent should be hidden or used in a fabric motif, as images sacred to the god.

Sunset is a beneficial time to begin, as it is the time to cast away pain and sorrow. Sunrise is a symbolic starting point—a ritual new beginning, a freeing and rejuvenation.

In particular, the tones of green should be used to represent hope, healing, love, and empathy. Emerald green emits the vibration of hope. Red, purple, and pink all send medicinal energies to immunological problems and ease mental stress. These stones should be attached or hidden in the seams: jet, garnet, clear quartz, turquoise. These are natural tranquilizers, emitting calming energy and magnifying beneficial effects of other magic components. Black jet is a stone specific to raising depression and is a traditional mourning jewel.

Use the ideograms for love, patience, courage, and enlightenment. These are qualities you will need to work through your loss and virtues that the viewer of the quilt should receive.

The following instructions are quoted from the NAMES Project Foundation information booklet regarding the quilt.

"All kinds of people have made panels for the NAMES Project AIDS Memorial Quilt, in a variety of colors, fabrics and styles. You do not have to be a professional artist or a sewing expert to create a moving personal tribute. It doesn't matter if you use paint or fine needle work; any remembrance is appropriate. You may choose to do a panel privately as a personal memorial to someone you've loved, but we encourage you to follow the traditions of old-fashioned sewing and quilting bees, by including friends, family, and co-workers.

Design the panel:
- Include the name of the friend or loved one you are remembering.

- Feel free to include additional information such as the dates of birth and death, and a hometown.

- Please limit each panel to one individual.

Choose your materials:
- Remember that the quilt is folded and unfolded many times, so durability is crucial.

- A medium weight, non-stretch fabric such as a cotton duck or poplin works best.

- Your design can be vertical or horizontal, but the finished, hemmed panel must be 3 feet by 6 feet—no more and no less. When you cut the fabric, leave an extra 2-3 inches on each side for a hem. If you can't hem it yourself, we'll do it for you.

- Batting for the panels is not necessary, but backing is recommended. Backing helps to keep panels clean when they are laid out on the ground. It also helps them retain the shape of the fabric.

To construct your panel you might want to use some of the following techniques:

Applique: Sew fabric letters and small mementos onto the background fabric. Do not rely on glue. It won't last.

Paint: Brush on textile paint or color-fast dye, or use an indelible ink pen. No "Puffy" paint; it's too sticky.

Stencil: Trace your design on to the fabric with a pencil, lift the stencil, then use a brush to apply textile paint or indelible markers.

Collage: Make sure that whatever materials you add to the panel won't tear the fabric (avoid glass and sequins for this reason), and be sure to avoid very bulky objects.

Photos: The best way to include photos or letters is to photocopy them onto iron-on transfers, iron them onto 100% cotton fabric and sew that fabric to the panel. You may also put the photo in clear plastic vinyl and sew it to the panel (off center so it avoids the fold.)

Some of the items included in the panels are burlap, bubble-wrap, love letters, hair, Mardi Gras masks, shirts, car keys, records, stuffed animals, jewelry, jeans, lace, leather, photos, merit badges and credit cards.

Contact The NAMES Project Foundation, 310 Townsend Street, Suite 310, San Francisco, CA, 94107 for more information."

The NAMES Project has continued to display the quilt since 1987. All or part of the quilt has appeared in over 1,000 displays, around the country. It has been displayed in schools, churches, malls, theaters, prisons, and museums.

There have been contributions of panels from thirty-nine countries and all the states. When an individual panel is received at the NAMES Foundation headquarters, it is examined for durability and reinforced if needed. When eight panels from the same region are collected, they are assembled into a 12-foot by 12-foot section. Each of these sections is then edged in canvas, brass grommets are added, and the section is numbered.

There are now over 30,899 individual panels, each panel measuring 3 feet by 6 feet.

Without the walkways between sections, the quilt would cover thirteen acres or twelve football fields. It weighs over 36 tons, not including the walkways.

The NAMES Project displays parts of the quilt approximately 200 times a year. The full quilt has grown too large for complete exhibition, other than in a large area such as the Capitol Mall in Washington, DC.

"Common Threads" is a video produced by the NAMES Project and available at video stores. If you feel inspired to produce a memorial panel, or want to understand the Project further, the video is a moving and informative production. Since 1987, the NAMES Project AIDS Memorial Quilt has grown from a neighborhood cause to an internationally recognized symbol of awareness, love, and hope.

Let not the waves of the sea separate us now,
and the years you have spent in our midst become a memory.

—Kahlil Gibran

Annotated Bibliography
and Suggested Resources

Aria, Barbara with R. Eng Gon. *The Spirit of the Chinese Character; Gifts from the Heart.* San Francisco: Chronicle Books, 1992.

This book explores the many meanings of forty fundamental ideograms of the Chinese language. These characters are thought to be spiritually inspired and artistically and culturally evocative.

Baker, Muriel and Margaret Lunt. *Blue and White; The Cotton Embroideries of Rural China.* New York: Scribner's, 1977.

Motifs and folklore of rural Chinese needlework.

Biedermann, Hans. *Dictionary of Symbolism.* New York: Meridian-Penguin, 1994.

An intriguing cross-cultural encyclopedic listing of commonly recurring motifs and their meanings.

Budapest, Zsuzanna. *The Grandmother of Time*. New York: Harper Collins, 1989.

A book of women's celebrations, spells, and sacred objects for each month of the year, integrating Wiccan spirituality into everyday life.

Buckland, Raymond. *Practical Candleburning Rituals*. St. Paul: Llewellyn, 1990.

A very complete explanation of uses of candles for magic.

Clark, Linda. *The Ancient Art of Color Therapy*. Old Greenwich, CN: Devin-Adair Co., 1975.

Use of colors to influence healthful living.

Cunningham, Scott. *Encyclopedia of Magical Herbs*. St Paul: Llewellyn, 1993.

Over 400 plants are discussed, with exact magical procedures for using them. Includes Latin nomenclature, cross-reference of folk names, listing of suppliers, glossary, annotated bibliography, and illustrations.

———. *Earth, Air, Fire and Water*. St Paul: Llewellyn, 1993.

Practical spells for contemporary folk magic, using the tools of the four natural elements of earth, air, fire and water.

———. *Earth Power*. St Paul: Llewellyn, 1994.

More than 100 spells, rituals and divinations for effective positive magic using the power and symbolism of Nature.

———. *Magical Herbalism*. St Paul: Llewellyn, 1993.

Step by step guidance to the preparation of herbs in incenses, amulets, and infusions; simple rituals and spells for every purpose. Help in tapping the power within us and in the natural objects in the world.

———. *Incense, Oils and Brews*. St. Paul: Llewellyn, 1993.

Composition of incense, blending of oils and herbal remedies, formulas and recipes for ritual soaps, brews, and powders. Detailed information on sources, ingredients, substitutions, a glossary, and basic principles of natural positive magic.

Cunningham, Scott and David Harrington. *The Magical Household; Empower Your Home with Love, Protection, Health, and Happiness*. St Paul: Llewellyn, 1990.

Magical folk lore from all over the world relating to the home. Techniques to bring out the special qualities of our daily surroundings. Kitchen magic, bath magic, door and pet magic.

———. *Spell Crafts; Creating Magical Objects*. St Paul: Llewellyn, 1994.

A modern guide to creating physical objects for the attainment of specific magical goals. How to imbue your hand crafts with specific energies for attracting a positive effect on your life, such as love, protection, or inner peace.

Dreher, Diane. *The Tao of Inner Peace*. New York: Harper Collins, 1990.

Applying Taoist principles to ourselves and the world around us. Inspiration and practical advice drawn from the Taoist principles of harmonious action, dynamic balance, and cosmic unity.

Gordon, Anne. *A Book of Saints*. New York: Harper Collins, 1994.

A short compendium of common and uncommon Christian saints and their attributes.

Gonzalez-Wippler, Migene. *The Complete Book of Talismans and Amulets*. St. Paul: Llewellyn, 1993.

History of amulets and talismans; how to construct them.

———. *Powers of the Orishas*. NY: Original Publications, 1992.

Introduction to the gods and goddesses of the Santeria religion.

Hamilton, Edith. *Mythology*. Boston: Little, Brown and Co., 1942.

Classic, easy to read presentation of Greek, Roman and Norse mythology. These tales are the foundation of world literature.

Hanyu, Guo. *Chinese Textile Designs*. UK: Viking-Penguin, 1993.

History, motifs and folk lore of Chinese textile design.

Huang, Kerson and Rosemary. *The I Ching*. New York: Workman Kowalchik, C. and Hylton, W. editors.

Rodale's Illustrated Encyclopedia of Herbs. (26th edition) Emmaus, PA: Rodale Press, 1987.

Extensively researched and lavishly illustrated, this volume features entries on more than 140 herbs. Culinary, medicinal, artistic, and household uses are included. Identification, cultivation, and storage are presented.

Keyte, Geoffrey. *The Mystical Crystal*. England: C.W. Daniel, 1993.

Founder of the Crystal Research Foundation, Mr. Keyte explains electro-crystal therapy, the origins of crystal therapy and its relation to personal energy centers.

Kuntz, George F. *The Curious Lore of Precious Stones*. New York: Dover. Leach, Marjorie. Guide to the Gods. Santa Barbara, CA: ABC-CLIO, 1992.

Comprehensive encyclopedic listing of gods, goddesses, and deified mortals of most world-wide cultures including Tibetan, African, Asian, American Indian and Polynesian.

McClun, Diana and Laura Nownes. *Quilts, Quilts, Quilts*. San Francisco: Quilt Digest Press, 1988.

A basic text on quiltmaking arranged in order of difficulty. Easy to follow; illustrated in color and with diagrams.

Mickaharic, Draja. *A Century of Spells*. York Beach, ME: Samuel Wieser, 1988.

An introduction and overview of natural magic methods.

The NAMES Project Foundation. *Information Handbooklet*, 1996.

For further information, see "Suggested Resources."

Rossbach, Sarah and Lin Yun. *Living Color; Master Lin Yun's Guide to Feng Shui and the Art of Color*. New York: Kodansha Int., 1994.

Introduction and explanation of the Chinese art and science of adjusting living space in order to be in harmony with the natural flow of geologic and mystic energies.

Sabrina, Lady. *Reclaiming the Power*. St. Paul: Llewellyn, 1992.

Practical magic; use of magic in everyday life.

Telesco, Patricia. *A Victorian Grimoire*. St. Paul: Llewellyn, 1992.

A study of Victorian era application of magic and common sense knowledge to every corner of daily life.

Suggested Resources

The NAMES Project Foundation.

For information on the AIDS/NAMES quilt, write to: The NAMES Project Foundation, 310 Townsend St, Suite 310, San Francisco, CA 94107

South East Art Quilters (SEA Q), B. W. Watler, 9400 NW 38th St, Hollywood, FL 33024

Internet: Art Quilt List, Hurricane Menu, Museum Menu.

Index

The Crafting & Use of Ritual Tools

Step-by-Step Instructions for Woodcrafting
Religious & Magical Implements

Eleanor and Philip Harris

Raise the power of your magical practice to new heights through the creation of your own ritual tools. Here is the first book of practical instructions for hand-crafting—from wood—a ritual staff, wand, rune set, ritual knife, and magical shield. From obtaining the desired raw materials to using your finished products in ritual, this book teaches beginning woodcrafters everything you need to enjoy the alchemical art of crafting sacred implements using tools found in most households. The techniques of carving, painting, wood branding, sanding, staining, and applying finish are explained in a simple "how-to" format.

From materials pulsing with the energy of nature, you can hand-craft implements of equal or better quality than the more expensive ones available for purchase. What's more, you can infuse them with your own personal energy, making them a sacred extension of your unique beliefs, practices, and personal symbolism.

1-56718-346-8, 240 pp., 6 x 9 $14.95

Mad About Mead

Nectar of the Gods

Pamela Spence

Mead—it was the elixir of red-bearded Vikings and sloe-eyed Sheba. Ancient peoples believed that drinking the fermented honey imparted the divine gifts of prophecy, poetry and fertility. Far from being an historical oddity, however, mead is now enjoying an international revival.

Mad About Mead is geared to those who are intrigued by the "idea" of mead as well as to those who actually make it. Written in a light-hearted, humorous style, it is an eclectic mix of history, mythology, rituals and instructions. The detailed recipe section has information about honey varieties, yeasts, equipment, and problem solving, plus a chapter on commercial mead production. You will find directions for brewing pumpkin mead (right in the pumpkin) alongside lab-tested recipes for melomel ... and recipes using bee pollen and forage fruit alongside recipes using commercial yeast energizers and acid blends. The resource section will point you to others who share the mead madness.

1-56718-683-1, 208 pp., 6 x 9, illus., softcover $12.95

To order, call 1–800–THE MOON
Prices subject to change without notice.

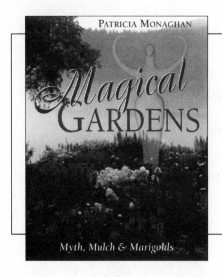

Magical Gardens

Myths, Mulch and Marigolds

Patricia Monaghan

Like ancient alchemists, gardeners transform common materials—seed, soil, sun and water—into the gold of beauty and nourishment. In the process, gardeners transform their own souls as well; time spent in the garden is a sacred time, a time of meditation and worship. For such gardeners, *Magical Gardens* offers insights in making a more conscious connection between soul and soil, between humus and the human spirit.

Plant an Angel Garden, which comes into its own in the moonlight, shining with its own secret radiance … or an Aphrodite's Bower, abundant with flowers and passion, crowded and dense with bloom … or a Sorcerer's Secret Garden, where in voluptuous privacy you can feel secure enough to envision utter freedom. Myths, meditations and magical rituals are combined with garden plans that honor the old divinities and the old ways.

1-56718-466-9, 192 pp., 8½ x 11, softcover $17.95

THE MAGICAL HOUSEHOLD

Empower Your Home with Love
Protection, Health and Happiness

Scott Cunningham and
David Harrington

Whether your home is a small apartment or a palatial mansion, you want it to be something special. Now it can be with *The Magical Household*. Learn how to make your home more than just a place to live. Turn it into a place of security, life, fun and magic. Here you will not find the complex magic of the ceremonial magician. Rather, you will learn simple, quick and effective magical spells that use nothing more than common items in your house: furniture, windows, doors, carpet, pets, etc. You will learn to take advantage of the intrinsic power and energy that is already in your home, waiting to be tapped. You will learn to make magic a part of your life. The result is a home that is safeguarded from harm and a place which will bring you happiness, health and more.

0-87542-124-5, 208 pp., 5¼ x 8, illus., softcover $9.95

Magical Needlework

35 Original Projects & Patterns

Dorothy Morrison

Creating beautiful and artistic handcrafts is in itself a magical act. Now, you can use your craft projects to further imbue your home with a magical atmosphere and evoke magical energy.

Magical Needlework explores the versatility of this magical art and offers a myriad of "hands-on" projects, ideas and patterns submitted by a wide spectrum of people within the spiritual community. You will discover the type of magical powers contains within various symbols, numbers, shapes, textures, stitches and weaves.

Sew a fairie dress for Midsummer Night's Eve and dancing in the moonlight ... safeguard your home with an herbal protection charm ... crochet a pentacle wallhanging ... quilt an herbal soap bag and infuse it with magical success ... knit a mediation mat for balance in your life ... and much, much more.

1-56718-470-7, 224 pp., 8½ x 10⅞, photos, illus., softcover $17.95

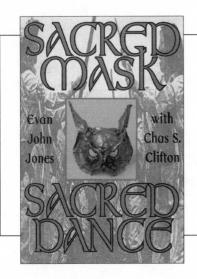

Sacred Mask Sacred Dance

Evan John Jones & Chas Clifton

Wearing a mask as an aid to moving toward the spirit of an animal or god is one of the world's oldest magical techniques. Now shamanically inclined Witches can incorporate masked workings into a Pagan form of consciousness alteration. The masks may represent different aspects within the Old Faith, becoming the faces of the minor gods and goddesses called upon within the cycle of the rites. This bold, new concept in ritual enables direct communion between the sacred dancer and these gods. The dramatic value of masked working is so strong because it is transpersonal; you present visual messages to one another with the masks and costumes that you wear. Sacred Mask, Sacred Dance discusses the power of the mask, the historical religious connection between masked rituals and the Underworld, and a discussion on trance itself.

1-56718-373-5, 224 pp., 7 x 10, illus., photos, softcover $19.95

Spell Crafts

Creating Magical Objects

Scott Cunningham
& David Harrington

Since early times, crafts have been intimately linked with spirituality. When a woman carefully shaped a water jar from the clay she'd gathered from a river bank, she was performing a spiritual practice. When crafts were used to create objects intended for ritual or that symbolized the Divine, the connection between the craftsperson and divinity grew more intense. Today, handcrafts can still be more than a pastime—they can be rites of power and honor; a religious ritual. After all, hands were our first magical tools.

Spell Crafts is a modern guide to creating physical objects for the attainment of specific magical goals. It is far different from magic books that explain how to use purchased magical tools. You will learn how to fashion spell brooms, weave wheat, dip candles, sculpt clay, mix herbs, bead sacred symbols and much more, for a variety of purposes. Whatever your craft, you will experience the natural process of moving energy from within yourself (or within natural objects) to create positive change.

0-87542-185-7, 224 pp., 5¼ x 8, illus., photos $10.00

To order, call 1–800–THE MOON
Prices subject to change without notice.